Sales Prospecting Made Simple:

Finding and Engaging Your Ideal Customers

Published by: John Messina

Copyright © 2024. All rights reserved.

You're welcome to enjoy this book, but please don't copy, share, or reproduce any part of it—whether by printing, scanning or any other method—without getting permission first from the author and publisher.

Disclaimer:

This book, *Sales Prospecting Made Simple*, was created with a lot of research, effort and attention to detail to provide you with practical tips and strategies for your business and MLM journey. AI was used to assist in the process and the content was carefully reviewed for accuracy and relevance.

The advice and examples are meant to be a helpful guide, but every MLM journey is unique. Feel free to adapt the information to fit your personal style and goals. The goal of this book is to support and inspire you as you work toward success in your MLM business.

Table of Contents

PREFACE: WHY PROSPECTING IS YOUR SUPERPOWER......... 4

INTRODUCTION: WHY SALES PROSPECTING MATTERS 9

CHAPTER 1: UNDERSTANDING YOUR IDEAL CUSTOMER 15

CHAPTER 2: THE ART OF STARTING A CONVERSATION 32

CHAPTER 3: BUILDING TRUST AND RAPPORT 48

CHAPTER 4: PROSPECTING ONLINE AND OFFLINE 64

CHAPTER 5: HANDLING OBJECTIONS LIKE A PRO 81

CHAPTER 6: MAINTAINING MOMENTUM AND GROWING YOUR NETWORK 96

CONCLUSION: PROSPECTING WITH PURPOSE................... 111

RESOURCE SECTION: PRACTICAL TOOLS FOR YOUR MLM JOURNEY.. 116

Preface: Why Prospecting is Your Superpower

If you're picking up this book, chances are you're part of the MLM world—or you're thinking about diving in. Whether you're just starting or you've been in the game for a while, one thing is certain: **sales prospecting is the lifeblood of your business.** Without it, even the best products, the most exciting business opportunities, and your hard work can fall flat.

When I first entered the MLM space, I was clueless. I didn't know how to approach people, what to say, or how to handle the inevitable rejections. At first, I thought prospecting was about pushing a product or convincing people to join a business opportunity. I soon discovered that this approach led to awkward conversations, frustrated friends, and doors closing left, right, and centre.

But then I had a lightbulb moment. Prospecting isn't about selling—it's about connecting. It's about building relationships, understanding needs, and offering solutions in a way that feels natural and authentic. Once I made that shift, everything changed. Conversations flowed more easily, objections became less intimidating, and my business began to grow.

This book is the guide I wish I had when I started. It's designed to make prospecting simple, approachable, and even fun!

Why I Wrote This Book

Let's be honest—prospecting can feel overwhelming at first. You might worry about coming across as pushy or "sales-y." Maybe you're afraid of rejection, or you simply don't know where to begin. That's exactly why I wrote *Sales Prospecting Made Simple*. This book is here to demystify the process and give you practical tools to start conversations, build trust, and grow your network—without losing your friends or your confidence.

I've broken the book into clear, actionable steps, with real-life examples and stories to bring it all to life. Whether you're chatting to someone at the local café, connecting online, or handling a tricky objection, you'll find guidance to help you navigate each step of the journey.

What You'll Learn

Here's a sneak peek of what's inside:

- **Understanding Your Ideal Customer** (Chapter 1): Before you start prospecting, you need to know *who* you're looking for. We'll dive into how to identify your ideal customer, where to find them, and how to connect in a meaningful way.

- **Starting Conversations with Confidence** (Chapter 2): Ever felt tongue-tied trying to start a conversation about your business? We'll explore practical ways to break the ice and get the conversation flowing naturally.

- **Building Trust and Rapport** (Chapter 3): People do business with those they like and trust. This chapter will show you how to build authentic relationships that lead to long-term success.

- **Prospecting Online and Offline** (Chapter 4): From social media strategies to turning everyday encounters into opportunities, we'll cover it all.

- **Handling Objections Like a Pro** (Chapter 5): Ah, objections—the part most people dread! In this chapter, I'll teach you how to handle objections with confidence and grace. Whether it's "I don't have the time" or "It's too expensive," you'll learn how to turn these challenges into opportunities.

- **Maintaining Momentum and Growing Your Network** (Chapter 6): Prospecting is a marathon, not a sprint. This chapter will help you stay consistent, nurture relationships, and keep growing your business over the long term.

Keeping It Real

I've made it a point to keep this book down-to-earth and relatable. You won't find any corporate jargon or overly complicated strategies here. Instead, I've packed it with practical tips and real-life examples you can apply straight away. Whether you're prospecting on Facebook, chatting to a friend, or following up with a potential lead, you'll find tools and techniques that fit into your everyday life.

To make it even easier, I've included stories from my own journey—mistakes, successes, and everything in between. You'll laugh at some of the blunders I've made along the way (like the time I tried to pitch my business opportunity at a family BBQ—don't do that, by the way).

A Note About Objections

Before we dive in, let me say a quick word about objections. If you're nervous about hearing "no" or dealing with pushback, you're not alone. It's a common fear for most people in sales, especially when they're just starting out.

Chapter 5 will arm you with the tools to handle objections confidently. But if you're really keen to master this skill, I highly recommend checking out my other book, **Overcoming Common Objections in MLM**. It's packed with scripts, strategies, and examples to help you tackle even the toughest objections with ease. Think of it as the perfect companion to this book!

Your Journey Starts Now

Prospecting isn't about being the loudest or most persuasive person in the room. It's about connecting with people in a way that feels natural, genuine, and mutually beneficial. It's about finding the right people—not convincing the wrong ones.

This book is your guide to making prospecting simple, effective, and even enjoyable. By the time you finish, you'll have the tools to start conversations, build trust, and grow your MLM business with confidence.

So, grab a cuppa, get comfortable, and let's dive in. Your MLM journey is about to get a whole lot easier—and a whole lot more rewarding.

Let's do this together!

Cheers,
John Messina

Introduction: Why Sales Prospecting Matters

Picture this: you've just joined an MLM company. You're excited, brimming with enthusiasm about the product or service you're offering and you genuinely believe it can change lives. You've got your starter kit, a few training sessions under your belt and maybe even a list of potential prospects to contact. But as the days pass, a creeping sense of uncertainty sets in.

You start to wonder, *Who should I talk to? What do I say? What if they think I'm pushy or, worse, just trying to make money off them?*

If this sounds familiar, you're not alone. In fact, I'd say just about every MLM rep has felt this way at some point. Sales prospecting can feel intimidating, even overwhelming, especially when you're new to the game. But here's the good news: it doesn't have to be.

In this book, we're going to take the mystery—and the fear—out of prospecting. I'll show you how to build authentic connections, start conversations that feel natural and engage with people in a way that's both effective and enjoyable. You'll learn practical tools and strategies to help you grow your network, find the right customers and ultimately, build a successful MLM business.

But before we dive into the "how," let's talk about why sales prospecting matters. Once you understand its importance, you'll see that it's not just a skill to learn—it's a superpower that can transform your business and your life.

A Story of Struggle and Success

Let me introduce you to Lisa. Lisa is a mum of two who joined an MLM company after falling in love with their health and wellness products. She had no prior experience in sales but was drawn to the flexibility and the idea of earning extra income while helping others improve their health.

At first, Lisa was on fire. She told her closest friends and family about the products and a few of them made purchases. That initial success gave her a boost of confidence, but soon, she hit a wall. Her friends had bought what they needed and her family wasn't interested in buying more.

Lisa began to panic. She thought, *Who else can I talk to? Everyone I know already knows what I'm doing. I don't want to annoy them or seem desperate.*

She tried reaching out to everybody she knew on social media but found herself fumbling for words. She didn't want to come across as pushy, so her messages were vague and unconvincing. Unsurprisingly, she didn't get many responses.

To make matters worse, Lisa started to dread the idea of prospecting. Every time she thought about reaching out to someone, she felt a knot in her stomach. She began to doubt herself and even considered quitting altogether.

Sound familiar?

Now, here's the turning point. Lisa decided to get some guidance. She reached out to her upline mentor, who shared a few simple strategies for effective prospecting. Lisa learned how to identify her ideal customer, start genuine conversations, and focus on building relationships instead of making quick sales.

With a renewed sense of purpose, Lisa approached prospecting differently. Instead of bombarding people with sales pitches, she took the time to understand their needs and interests. She learned to ask questions, listen actively and offer solutions that genuinely aligned with what they were looking for.

Over time, Lisa's confidence grew. She started seeing better results—not just in sales but in the quality of her interactions. She built a loyal customer base and even began to attract new team members who were inspired by her approach.

Today, Lisa's MLM business is thriving. She credits her success to mastering the art of prospecting—and more importantly, to shifting her mindset from "selling" to "connecting."

Why Prospecting Matters

Lisa's story illustrates a simple but powerful truth: **sales prospecting is the foundation of a successful MLM business.**

Think of prospecting as planting seeds. Each conversation you have, each relationship you build, is a seed that has the potential to grow into something amazing. Some seeds will sprout quickly, while others might take time. And yes, some won't grow at all. But the more seeds you plant, the greater your chances of success.

Here's the thing: MLM isn't just about selling products. It's about solving problems, meeting needs and building a community of people who trust and value what you have to offer. And none of that happens without prospecting.

When done right, prospecting isn't about pushing people to buy something they don't need. It's about finding the right people—the ones who truly benefit from your product or opportunity—and connecting with them in a way that feels natural and authentic.

Shifting Your Mindset

One of the biggest barriers to successful prospecting is fear. Fear of rejection, fear of being judged, fear of coming across as pushy. But here's the truth: those fears often come from a misunderstanding of what prospecting is all about.

Prospecting isn't about convincing someone to buy something or join your team. It's about starting a conversation and exploring whether there's a good fit. When you approach prospecting with the mindset of helping rather than selling, everything changes.

Instead of thinking, *What can I get out of this conversation?* ask yourself, *How can I add value to this person's life?*

This simple shift in mindset can make all the difference. It takes the pressure off you and makes the interaction more enjoyable for both you and your prospect.

The Practical Side of Prospecting

Of course, mindset is only part of the equation. You also need practical tools and strategies to make prospecting work. That's what this book is all about.

In the chapters ahead, you'll learn how to:

- Identify your ideal customer and understand their needs.
- Start conversations that feel natural and engaging.

- Build trust and rapport with prospects.
- Handle objections with confidence and ease.
- Leverage social media and offline interactions to expand your network.

You'll also find plenty of real-life examples, relatable stories, and actionable tips to help you put these strategies into practice. Whether you're chatting with someone at the local park, connecting with a potential lead on Facebook, or following up with a previous customer, you'll have the tools you need to prospect with confidence.

Your Journey Starts Here

As you read this book, I want you to remember one thing: prospecting is a skill and like any skill, it gets easier with practice. You don't have to be perfect. You just have to start.

It's okay to make mistakes. It's okay to feel nervous. What matters is that you take action. Each conversation, no matter how small, is a step forward.

By the time you finish this book, you'll have a clear roadmap to prospecting success. You'll know how to connect with people authentically, handle objections gracefully and grow your MLM business in a way that feels true to you.

So, let's get started. Your future customers—and your future success—are waiting.

Chapter 1: Understanding Your Ideal Customer

Who Are They, Really?

When I first started in MLM, I was told to create a list of everyone I knew. Friends, family, colleagues, neighbours—the works. The idea was simple: reach out to as many people as possible and hope someone would bite. For a while, I followed this advice to the letter. I made phone calls, sent messages, and even tried a few awkward pitches at social gatherings.

But here's what happened. Most of the time, the people I approached weren't interested. Some were polite but declined, while others made it clear they didn't want to be bothered. A few even asked me not to bring up "that sales stuff" ever again. It was disheartening, to say the least.

What I didn't realise back then was that I was trying to sell to *everyone* and in doing so, I was actually connecting with *no one*. The truth is, not everyone is your ideal customer. And that's okay. In fact, it's a good thing. Once you figure out who your ideal customer really is, you can focus your time and energy on the people who are most likely to benefit from what you're offering—and who are most likely to say yes.

Defining the "Ideal Customer"

So, who is your ideal customer? They're not just anyone who might buy your product or join your team. They're the people who genuinely need what you have to offer, who resonate with your message and who align with your values.

Let's take an example from the world of health and wellness. Imagine you're promoting a range of natural supplements. Your ideal customer isn't just "anyone who wants to be healthy." That's far too broad. Instead, think about the specific problems your products solve. Are they designed for busy mums looking for an energy boost? Athletes who want to recover faster? People in their 40s and 50s who are starting to think about long-term health?

The more specific you can be, the better. When you know exactly who you're trying to reach, it's easier to tailor your message, approach the right people and have conversations that truly resonate.

For instance, one of my team members, Helen, used to struggle with this. She was promoting skincare products and kept telling me, "Everyone has skin, so everyone is a potential customer!" While technically true, this mindset wasn't helping her connect with anyone.

We sat down and talked about what made her products unique. Helen realised they were particularly beneficial for people with sensitive skin or those looking for natural alternatives to harsh chemicals. Once she identified her ideal customer as women in their 30s and 40s who cared about clean beauty, everything changed. Her conversations became more focused, her approach felt more authentic and her sales started to pick up.

Moving Beyond Generic Target Markets

It's tempting to rely on generic labels like "women aged 25-45" or "people who want to make extra money." But these broad categories don't give you enough insight into who your ideal customer really is.

Think about it: not all women aged 25-45 have the same needs, interests or goals. Some might be busy professionals juggling work and family, while others might be new mums navigating sleepless nights. Their challenges are different, and so are the ways your product or opportunity could help them.

To move beyond generic target markets, start by asking yourself these questions:

- What problems does my product or service solve?
- Who is most likely to have these problems?
- What are their goals, values, and priorities?

The more you dig into these questions, the clearer your ideal customer will become. And once you have that clarity, everything from your messaging to your prospecting strategy will fall into place.

For example, I once worked with a team member, Peter, who was promoting a fitness program. At first, he struggled because he was targeting "people who want to get fit." But after some reflection, Peter realised his program was especially appealing to men in their 30s and 40s who didn't have time for the gym but wanted to stay active. Armed with this understanding, Peter shifted his focus and his business started to thrive.

The Role of Empathy and Active Listening

Now, here's the secret sauce: understanding your ideal customer isn't just about demographics or interests. It's about empathy. It's about stepping into their shoes, seeing the world through their eyes and understanding what they truly need.

Empathy is what transforms a sales pitch into a meaningful conversation. It's what helps you connect with people on a human level, rather than just seeing them as potential buyers.

Let me share a story. A few years ago, I was prospecting for a wellness product that helped with stress and sleep. One of the people I reached out to was a friend of a friend, Maria, who worked as a nurse.

When I first messaged Maria, I didn't jump straight into talking about the product. Instead, I asked her how she was doing. She told me she was struggling with long shifts, stress, and sleepless nights. I listened, really listened and let her share what was on her mind.

It wasn't until later in the conversation that I mentioned the product. I said something like, "Maria, I couldn't help but think of you when I came across this product. It's designed to help with stress and sleep and I think it might be a good fit for what you're going through. No pressure, of course—just thought I'd share it with you."

Maria ended up trying the product and she became one of my most loyal customers. But more importantly, we built a genuine connection. She told me later that what stood out to her wasn't the product—it was the fact that I took the time to listen and understand her needs.

This is the power of empathy and active listening. It's not about pushing your agenda. It's about being present, asking the right questions and really hearing what the other person is saying.

Bringing It All Together

Understanding your ideal customer is the foundation of successful prospecting. It's about more than just knowing who they are—it's about understanding their challenges, their goals and how you can help them.

As you go through this book, I encourage you to keep empathy at the heart of everything you do. Take the time to really get to know your prospects, ask thoughtful questions and listen with an open mind.

When you approach prospecting with this mindset, something amazing happens. Instead of feeling like a chore, it becomes an opportunity to connect, to serve and to make a difference in people's lives. And that's what MLM is all about.

So, who is your ideal customer? It's time to find out. Let's dive in.

Researching Your Ideal Customer

Once you have a clear picture of who your ideal customer is, the next step is figuring out where to find them and how to understand their needs, habits and aspirations. The good news? You're living in a time where gathering this information is easier than ever, thanks to the incredible tools at your fingertips. Social media, in particular, can be a goldmine of insights if you know how to use it effectively. But as with anything, there are right ways and wrong ways to go about it.

In this section, we'll explore how to use social media to understand your ideal customer better, how to uncover their pain points and aspirations and how to avoid common mistakes like stereotyping or jumping to conclusions.

Using Social Media to Understand Habits and Interests

Social media is where people let their guard down and show their true selves. It's where they share their likes, dislikes, struggles and successes. For someone in MLM, it's an invaluable resource for understanding your ideal customer.

Let's say your product is a range of eco-friendly cleaning supplies. By spending time on social media, you can identify people who are passionate about sustainability, families looking for safer alternatives or even parents concerned about reducing toxins in their homes.

But how do you find these people? Start by exploring groups, hashtags and communities that align with your niche. For instance, if your product targets health-conscious individuals, look for Facebook groups centred around clean eating, wellness or fitness. On Instagram, search for hashtags like #sustainableliving or #healthylifestyle. LinkedIn, too, can be a great place to connect with professionals who might resonate with your message.

Once you're in these spaces, observe. What kind of content are people posting? What questions are they asking? What challenges are they sharing? This isn't about jumping in with a sales pitch—it's about listening and learning.

Take, for example, a former team member of mine, Julie, who was promoting a skincare product. She joined a few Facebook groups for women dealing with sensitive skin. Instead of immediately promoting her product, she spent time engaging in discussions, answering questions and sharing tips. Through this process, she not only learned more about her ideal customer's struggles but also built trust and credibility within the group.

Eventually, when Julie did mention her product, it didn't feel like a sales pitch. It felt like a natural extension of the conversations she was already having. And because she had taken the time to understand the group's needs, her suggestions were well-received.

Spotting Potential Pain Points and Aspirations

Every ideal customer has two sides to their story: the challenges they face (pain points) and the goals they want to achieve (aspirations). Understanding both is key to connecting with them on a deeper level.

Let me share a real-life example. I once worked with a health product that supported weight management and energy levels. One of my prospects, Emma, was a busy mum of three who often felt exhausted and struggled to maintain a healthy routine. Her pain points were clear: she was tired, short on time and felt overwhelmed by conflicting health advice.

But Emma also had aspirations. She wanted more energy to keep up with her kids, to feel confident in her own skin and to set a good example for her family.

By identifying both her challenges and her goals, I was able to position the product not just as a solution to her problems but as a stepping stone toward the life she wanted. I didn't approach Emma with a one-size-fits-all pitch. Instead, I said something like, "Emma, I know you're juggling so much right now, and it's hard to find time for yourself. This might not be for everyone, but I've been using a product that's really helped me feel more energised and balanced. Would you like to hear more about it?"

Notice the difference? It wasn't about selling—it was about offering a solution tailored to her specific needs.

To spot these pain points and aspirations in your ideal customers, pay attention to what they're saying on social media or in everyday conversations. What are they complaining about? What are they celebrating? What are their dreams, goals, and fears?

The key is to approach this with genuine curiosity. When you focus on understanding people rather than selling to them, you'll find opportunities to help in ways that feel authentic and natural.

Avoiding Pitfalls Like Stereotyping or Assumptions

Now, here's where it gets tricky. As you start researching your ideal customer, it's easy to fall into the trap of stereotyping or making assumptions. This can not only hurt your credibility but also damage potential relationships before they even begin.

For instance, just because someone is a young mum doesn't automatically mean they'll be interested in your product. Or just because someone posts about fitness doesn't mean they're looking for a new supplement. Assumptions can lead to awkward conversations and missed opportunities.

A good rule of thumb is to treat every prospect as an individual. Instead of assuming you know what they need, ask questions. Instead of jumping to conclusions, listen to what they're actually saying.

One of my early mistakes in MLM was assuming that people in my network who shared motivational quotes or talked about self-improvement would automatically be interested in my business opportunity. I reached out to a few of them with messages like, "I saw your post about personal growth, and I think you'd love this business opportunity I'm part of!"

To my surprise, most of them weren't interested. In fact, a few told me they felt like I was trying to fit them into a box that didn't match who they really were. It was a humbling lesson, but an important one.

Since then, I've made it a point to approach prospects with an open mind. Instead of assuming I know what they want, I ask questions like, "What's been going well for you lately?" or "What are you focusing on right now?" These conversations often reveal insights I wouldn't have uncovered otherwise—and they help me build trust and rapport in the process.

Putting It All Together

Researching your ideal customer is about more than just gathering data—it's about truly understanding the people you want to connect with. Social media gives you a window into their world, showing you their habits, interests and challenges. By listening carefully, you can uncover their pain points and aspirations, allowing you to position your product or opportunity as a genuine solution.

But as you do this, remember to stay curious and open-minded. Avoid the temptation to stereotype or make assumptions, and instead focus on building real relationships.

When you take the time to understand your ideal customer, you're not just setting yourself up for better conversations—you're laying the foundation for a more successful and fulfilling MLM journey. And that, my friend, is what this business is all about.

Building a Customer Avatar

If understanding your ideal customer is the foundation of your MLM success, then building a customer avatar is like drawing a detailed map to guide your efforts. It's the difference between wandering aimlessly and knowing exactly where you're headed. When you have a clear picture of who you're trying to reach, you can craft messages that resonate, approach the right people and connect in ways that feel natural and authentic.

But what exactly is a customer avatar? How do you create one? And why is it so important for your MLM business? Let's break it down.

What is a Customer Avatar and Why It's Essential?

A customer avatar is a detailed, almost lifelike profile of your ideal customer. It goes beyond basic demographics like age and gender to include their habits, values, challenges and aspirations. Essentially, it's a representation of the type of person who would be most interested in and benefit most from your product or opportunity.

Why is it essential? Well, when you know exactly who you're talking to, everything becomes easier. Your messaging becomes clearer, your prospecting efforts more focused and your interactions more meaningful. Instead of trying to appeal to everyone (and ending up appealing to no one), you can target your efforts where they'll have the greatest impact.

Imagine you're promoting a line of eco-friendly cleaning products. If you don't have a clear customer avatar, you might try to sell to anyone who cleans their house. But when you take the time to build an avatar, you might realise your ideal customer is a busy mum in her 30s who's passionate about sustainability and worried about exposing her kids to harsh chemicals. Suddenly, you know exactly what to say and where to find her.

Step-by-Step Guide to Creating a Vivid, Actionable Avatar

Building a customer avatar is like putting together a puzzle. Each piece adds depth and clarity to the picture, helping you see your ideal customer as a real person rather than just a vague concept. Here's how to do it:

1. **Start with the Basics**
   Begin by answering some fundamental questions:
   - How old is your ideal customer?
   - Are they male or female, or does gender not matter?
   - What's their marital or family status?
   - What do they do for a living?

These details might seem simple, but they lay the groundwork for a more detailed profile.

2. **Dig into Their Challenges and Aspirations**
   What problems are they facing that your product or opportunity can solve? Are they looking for more energy, better skin, extra income or a supportive community? At the same time, think about their goals and dreams. What do they want to achieve?

3. **Understand Their Habits and Interests**
   What does their daily life look like? Do they spend time on social media? If so, which platforms? Are they into fitness, travel, or wellness? Knowing their habits

and interests helps you figure out where and how to connect with them.

4. **Explore Their Values and Beliefs**
What matters most to them? Are they driven by family, health, personal growth or financial security? Understanding their values gives you insight into what motivates them and how you can align your messaging with what they care about.

5. **Give Your Avatar a Name and Story**
To make your avatar feel real, give them a name and create a short backstory. This might sound silly, but it helps you visualise them as a real person.

Real-Life Example of a Completed Customer Avatar

Let's bring this to life with an example. Imagine you're promoting a line of premium nutritional supplements. After going through the steps above, you create the following customer avatar:

Name: Sandra
Age: 35
Family Status: Married, mum to two kids aged 5 and 8
Occupation: Part-time teacher
Location: Suburban Melbourne

Challenges:
Sandra struggles with low energy and feels like she's constantly juggling work, family and household

responsibilities. She's often too tired to exercise or cook healthy meals and worries about setting a bad example for her kids.

Aspirations:
Sandra dreams of feeling more energised and confident in her own skin. She wants to prioritise her health so she can keep up with her kids and enjoy an active lifestyle with her family.

Habits and Interests:
Sandra spends a lot of time on Instagram, where she follows fitness influencers and mum bloggers. She's a member of a local Facebook group for mums and occasionally attends yoga classes when her schedule allows.

Values:
Sandra values family, health and sustainability. She's willing to invest in products that are natural, eco-friendly, and effective.

Backstory:
Sandra's mornings start early, packing lunches and getting her kids ready for school before heading to her part-time job. By the afternoon, she's drained and relies on coffee to push through the rest of the day. She's tried other health products before but found them complicated or ineffective. She's looking for something simple and convenient that fits into her busy life.

With this customer avatar in mind, you can tailor your approach. Instead of sending a generic message about your supplements, you might say something like:

"Hi Sandra, I noticed you're passionate about health and family, and I couldn't help but think of you when I started using this new product. It's helped me feel more energised and balanced, even on my busiest days. Would you like to know more about it? No pressure—just thought I'd share!"

How a Customer Avatar Transforms Your MLM Business

When you have a clear customer avatar, prospecting becomes more intentional and less overwhelming. Instead of feeling like you're grasping at straws, you know exactly who to reach out to and how to connect with them.

It's important to remember that your avatar isn't set in stone. As you gain more experience and interact with different customers, your understanding of your ideal customer might evolve. That's a good thing—it means you're growing and learning.

Building a customer avatar takes a bit of effort upfront, but it pays off in spades. It helps you focus your time and energy on the people who are most likely to resonate with your message, making your prospecting efforts more efficient and more rewarding.

So, take the time to create your customer avatar. Bring them to life with a name, a story and a detailed profile. Picture them in your mind every time you craft a message, start a conversation, or share your product or opportunity.

When you know exactly who you're talking to, you're no longer just selling—you're connecting. And that's where the magic happens.

Chapter 2: The Art of Starting a Conversation

Getting Comfortable with Rejection

Rejection. The word alone is enough to make most people squirm. It's one of the biggest hurdles in MLM and yet, it's a part of the journey for anyone involved in sales. Whether it's a polite "no, thank you" or a door metaphorically slammed in your face, rejection can feel personal and discouraging. But here's the thing: rejection is not a reflection of your worth or abilities. It's simply part of the process. And the sooner you learn to reframe it, the easier and even more productive it becomes.

When I first started in MLM, I hated rejection. Every "no" felt like a personal failure. I remember one of my first cold pitches vividly. I'd messaged an old Uni buddy, excitedly telling her about the opportunity I was involved in. Her response? "Thanks, but I'm not interested. And honestly, I'd appreciate it if you didn't message me about this again."

I was gutted. I read her message over and over, replaying the conversation in my head and wondering what I'd done wrong.

For days, I avoided prospecting altogether, paralysed by the fear of hearing another "no." But eventually, I realised that if I wanted to succeed, I had to change how I thought about rejection.

Reframing Rejection as Learning

One of the most important lessons I've learned is that rejection isn't about you—it's about the other person's circumstances, priorities or timing. Maybe they're overwhelmed with work or family. Maybe they've had a bad experience with MLM in the past. Or maybe they're simply not interested right now. Whatever the reason, it's rarely personal.

Once I started seeing rejection as feedback rather than failure, it became less intimidating. Every "no" became an opportunity to reflect and improve. Did I approach the conversation in the right way? Was I clear about the value I was offering? Did I choose the right time to reach out?

For example, after that awkward pitch to my Uni friend, I realised my message had been too abrupt. I hadn't taken the time to reconnect or gauge her interest before diving into the opportunity. So, I adjusted my approach. Instead of leading with my pitch, I started with a friendly message to catch up and build rapport. While not every conversation led to a "yes," I noticed a significant improvement in how people responded.

Rejection can also teach you resilience. The more you experience it, the less it stings. Over time, you realise that a "no" isn't the end of the world—it's just part of the process.

Funny Real-Life Stories of Awkward MLM Pitches

If you've ever botched a pitch, you're not alone. Trust me, we've all been there. And sometimes, the best way to deal with rejection is to laugh about it.

I remember one particularly cringeworthy moment early in my MLM career. I'd recently joined a company promoting skincare products and was determined to make a sale at a family BBQ. In my eagerness, I approached my cousin's girlfriend, a dermatologist. Without thinking, I launched into a pitch about how these products were revolutionising skincare.

She listened politely but then said, "That's great, but as a dermatologist, I prefer to recommend products based on clinical studies and peer-reviewed research." I was mortified. Not only had I failed to make a sale, but I'd also completely misjudged my audience.

Looking back, it's hilarious. At the time, it was a valuable lesson: know your audience and pick your moments. Not every interaction is an opportunity for a pitch and that's okay.

Another classic story comes from a friend of mine, who accidentally sent a prospecting message meant for one person to her entire contact list. It included a personalised greeting, so dozens of people received a message that began with the wrong name. While she received plenty of "no thanks" replies, she also got a few chuckles and even a couple of curious responses. She turned the experience into a joke, apologised for the mix-up, and ended up making a sale to someone she never would've thought to approach otherwise.

These moments remind us that rejection and missteps are part of the journey. The key is to learn from them, laugh about them, and keep moving forward.

Building Resilience: Tips from Psychology

Resilience is the ability to bounce back from setbacks and it's a skill you can develop. In MLM, resilience is your armour against the inevitable ups and downs of prospecting.

One of the most effective ways to build resilience is to reframe how you think about rejection. Psychologists often talk about the concept of *growth mindset*—the belief that challenges and failures are opportunities to grow rather than reasons to give up. When you approach rejection with a growth mindset, you see it as a stepping stone rather than a stumbling block.

For example, let's say you reach out to someone about your product, and they respond with a firm "no." Instead of thinking, *I'm terrible at this, I'll never succeed,* try asking yourself, *What can I learn from this? Could I have approached the conversation differently? Is there a better way to explain the value of my product?*

Another powerful tool is practising self-compassion. It's easy to be hard on yourself after a rejection, but beating yourself up only makes it harder to keep going. Instead, treat yourself with the same kindness and understanding you'd offer a friend. Remind yourself that rejection is normal and it doesn't define your worth or potential.

One strategy that helped me was keeping a "wins journal." For every rejection I received, I made a point to write down a win—whether it was a positive conversation, a small sale or even just the fact that I'd taken action. Over time, this practice shifted my focus from what wasn't working to what was.

Finally, resilience comes from staying connected to your "why." Why did you join this MLM in the first place? What are your goals and dreams? When rejection feels overwhelming, reconnecting with your purpose can give you the strength to keep going. For me, it was the desire to create more freedom and flexibility in my life while helping others do the same. Keeping that vision in mind helped me push through the tough moments.

Turning Rejection into a Strength

The reality is, rejection is part of prospecting and you can't avoid it. But you can change how you respond to it. When you see rejection as a chance to learn, laugh and grow, it becomes less of a roadblock and more of a stepping stone.

You'll make mistakes. You'll have awkward conversations. You'll hear "no" more times than you can count. But every time you push through, you're building your resilience and sharpening your skills.

Remember, rejection isn't about you—it's about the other person's circumstances or priorities. And every "no" brings you closer to a "yes." So embrace the process, learn from each experience and keep moving forward. Because the more comfortable you become with rejection, the more unstoppable you'll be.

First Impressions Count

When it comes to prospecting, the first few moments of a conversation are critical. It's in those moments that people decide whether they feel comfortable with you, whether they trust you and whether they're interested in hearing more. No pressure, right?

But here's the thing: making a great first impression isn't about being perfect or having a rehearsed speech. It's about coming across as authentic, approachable and genuinely interested in the other person. When you focus on connection rather than perfection, those initial interactions become much easier—and much more enjoyable.

How to Come Across as Authentic and Approachable

Think back to a time when someone tried to sell you something. If they came across as overly rehearsed, pushy or insincere, you probably tuned out pretty quickly. But if they were warm, genuine, and genuinely interested in helping you, chances are you gave them your attention.

The same principle applies to prospecting. People can sense when you're being authentic and they're far more likely to engage with you if they feel like you're speaking from the heart rather than following a script.

For me, the shift from nervous to natural happened when I stopped trying to impress people and started focusing on connection. Instead of worrying about what to say, I focused on being present, listening and approaching each conversation with curiosity.

For example, if I was meeting someone new at an event, I wouldn't jump straight into talking about my product or opportunity. Instead, I'd start with something simple like, "Hi, I don't think we've met yet—I'm [Your Name]. What brings you here today?" That small, friendly question often opened the door to a relaxed conversation where I could learn more about the other person and look for ways to connect.

The same applies online. If you're reaching out to someone on social media, avoid sending a generic message like, "Hi, I have a great business opportunity for you." Instead, take a few moments to look at their profile and find something you genuinely admire or have in common. Maybe they posted a picture of a recent trip, or they shared something about their fitness journey. A thoughtful opening message could be, "Hi [Name], I just saw your post about [topic]. I love that—I've been wanting to visit [place] too! How was your trip?"

When you show genuine interest in the other person, you set the stage for a meaningful connection.

Crafting a Simple, Engaging Opening Line

A great opening line doesn't have to be complicated. In fact, the simpler, the better. The goal is to start the conversation on a positive note and make the other person feel comfortable.

Here are a few examples that have worked well for me:

- **At a networking event:** "Hi, I'm [Your Name]. What brought you here today?"

- **In a social setting:** "Hi, I'm [Your Name]. How do you know [mutual friend]?"

- **Online:** "Hi [Name], I noticed your post about [topic]—it really resonated with me. How are you finding [related experience]?"

The key is to make your opening line relevant to the situation and the person you're speaking with. Avoid jumping straight into a pitch or overwhelming them with information. Remember, your goal at this stage is to build rapport, not close a deal.

When I first started, I made the mistake of trying to fit too much into my opening lines. I'd say something like, "Hi, I'm [Your Name], and I wanted to tell you about this amazing product I'm working with—it's perfect for [list of benefits]!" Not surprisingly, most people either politely declined or ignored me altogether.

Once I simplified my approach, everything changed. Starting with a friendly question or observation allowed the conversation to flow naturally, and I found it much easier to transition into talking about my product or opportunity when the time was right.

Role-Playing Exercises to Nail Your First Interactions

Practice might not make perfect, but it certainly makes better. Role-playing is a fantastic way to build confidence and refine your approach before you engage with real prospects.

Here's how you can get started:

Step 1: Choose a Practice Partner
Find someone you trust—maybe a friend, family member or fellow MLM rep—and ask them to role-play with you. Make sure they're comfortable giving you honest feedback.

Step 2: Create Realistic Scenarios
Think about the types of interactions you're likely to have, whether it's striking up a conversation at a social event, reaching out to someone online or following up with a

previous lead. Set the scene and take turns playing both roles.

For example, if you're practising an online message, your partner might pretend to be a busy parent you've connected with on Facebook. You can craft and deliver your opening message, and they can respond as a prospect might.

Step 3: Reflect and Adjust
After each role-play, discuss what worked well and what could be improved. Did your opening line feel natural? Were you able to establish a connection? Did you transition smoothly into the conversation?

One thing I found incredibly helpful was recording myself during role-plays. Listening back allowed me to catch things I might not have noticed in the moment, like using too many filler words or sounding overly formal.

Step 4: Practice in Real Life
Once you've gained confidence through role-playing, start applying what you've learned in real-life interactions. Remember, every conversation is a chance to improve, so don't be afraid to make mistakes.

For instance, when I was practising my in-person approach, I made a point of starting conversations with strangers in everyday situations—at the gym, in line at the coffee shop or even waiting for the bus. These low-stakes interactions helped me refine my opening lines and become more comfortable striking up conversations.

41

Putting It All Together

First impressions matter, but they don't have to be intimidating. When you approach conversations with authenticity, craft a simple and engaging opening line and practice your interactions through role-playing, you set yourself up for success.

Remember, the goal isn't to deliver a perfect pitch—it's to connect with people in a way that feels natural and genuine. When you focus on building rapport and showing interest in the other person, the rest will follow.

So, whether you're starting a conversation at a networking event, catching up with an old friend online, or introducing yourself to someone new, take a deep breath, smile and let your authenticity shine. At the end of the day, people aren't just buying a product or joining a business—they're connecting with *you*.

Mastering Small Talk

Small talk often gets a bad rap. For many, it feels awkward, shallow or even like a waste of time. But when it comes to MLM prospecting, small talk is anything but trivial. It's the bridge that connects you to your prospects, laying the foundation for trust and rapport. When done right, it sets the stage for meaningful conversations—and eventually, potential business opportunities.

But mastering small talk isn't just about knowing what to say. It's about approaching conversations with genuine curiosity, finding common ground and avoiding anything that feels forced or "sales-y."

Why Small Talk is Crucial in Relationship-Building

Imagine meeting someone at a social event and their first words are, "Hi, I'd love to sell you something!" You'd probably run for the nearest exit. That's because relationships—whether personal or professional—are built on connection, not transactions. Small talk is the first step in creating that connection.

Think of small talk as a way to ease into deeper conversations. It's like warming up before a workout; it prepares the ground for trust to grow. In MLM, where relationships are everything, small talk gives you the chance to show your personality, understand your prospect better, and create a comfortable space where they feel valued and heard.

One of the biggest mistakes I made early in my MLM journey was skipping small talk altogether. I'd jump straight into a conversation about my product or opportunity, thinking I was being efficient. But instead of engaging people, I often left them feeling overwhelmed or turned off. It wasn't until I started embracing small talk—learning to relax and enjoy the process—that I began to see real results.

Small talk doesn't have to be superficial or meaningless. In fact, it's often in these seemingly casual conversations that you uncover the insights and shared interests that lead to genuine connections.

How to Connect Through Shared Interests

Finding common ground is one of the quickest ways to build rapport. People naturally gravitate towards those they feel they have something in common with, so identifying shared interests can help a conversation flow more naturally.

For example, let's say you're chatting with someone at a neighbourhood BBQ. You notice they're wearing a sports team cap. Instead of jumping straight into a pitch, you could start with, "I see you're a [team name] fan. How do you think they'll go this season?" This simple question shows interest in something they care about and opens the door to a relaxed, enjoyable conversation.

The same principle applies online. If you're connecting with someone on social media, take a moment to look at their profile. Do they post about travel, fitness or a particular hobby? Mention something specific to show you've taken the time to learn about them. For example: "Hi [Name], I couldn't help but notice your post about hiking in the Blue Mountains. I went there last year—such a stunning place! Do you go hiking often?"

A great example from my own experience came when I struck up a conversation with a fellow parent at my child's school sports day. We started chatting about the chaos of juggling work and kids' schedules, and before I knew it, we were laughing about shared experiences. Eventually, the conversation turned naturally to what I did for work and she became one of my most loyal customers—not because I pushed a product but because we'd built a genuine connection first.

Avoiding "Sales-y" Vibes and Being Genuinely Curious

One of the fastest ways to kill a conversation is to make it feel transactional. If your prospect senses that you're only talking to them because you want to sell something, they'll likely shut down. That's why it's so important to lead with curiosity rather than an agenda.

Being genuinely curious means asking open-ended questions, actively listening and showing interest in the other person's life and experiences. Instead of steering the conversation toward your product or opportunity, let it flow naturally. If the topic comes up, great. If it doesn't, that's okay too—remember, building relationships takes time.

Here's a quick tip: focus on *them*, not you. People love to talk about themselves and when you give them the space to do so, they'll leave the conversation feeling heard and valued. For example, instead of saying, "I've been using this amazing product that gives me so much energy," try asking, "What's been working for you lately to stay energised? I know it can be a challenge when life's so busy."

Avoiding "sales-y" vibes also means paying attention to your tone and body language. A relaxed, friendly approach will always feel more genuine than a rehearsed or overly enthusiastic pitch. Smile, make eye contact and let the conversation unfold at its own pace.

I once made the mistake of bringing up my MLM opportunity too early with a neighbour. We'd been chatting about the struggles of balancing work and family, and instead of staying in the moment, I blurted out, "You know, I've got this great business opportunity that might help you earn extra income." Her reaction was polite but distant and I realised I'd misread the situation. If I'd waited, built more trust, and let her express interest first, the outcome might have been very different.

Bringing it All Together

Mastering small talk isn't about memorising clever lines or controlling the conversation. It's about being present, curious and open to connection. When you approach small talk with the intention of getting to know the other person rather than pushing your agenda, it transforms from a dreaded chore into an enjoyable experience.

Here's what I've learned: every conversation, no matter how small, is an opportunity to build a relationship. Whether you're chatting with someone at the gym, striking up a conversation at a café or connecting with a friend of a friend on social media, small talk lays the groundwork for trust and understanding.

And when trust and understanding are in place, the door naturally opens to share your product or opportunity—not as a pitch but as a solution that fits their needs. So, embrace small talk. Take the time to find common ground, ask thoughtful questions and listen with genuine interest. Because when people feel seen and valued, they're far more likely to engage with what you have to offer.

In the end, small talk isn't small at all—it's the start of something bigger. And that's where your MLM journey truly begins.

Chapter 3: Building Trust and Rapport

Why Trust Matters

In the world of MLM, trust isn't just a nice-to-have—it's the foundation on which your entire business rests. Without trust, even the most well-crafted pitches or the best products in the world won't get you far. Yet, if we're being honest, MLM doesn't always have the best reputation when it comes to trust. Many people have had experiences with pushy reps or overblown promises that didn't deliver, creating what some call the "trust deficit" in MLM.

If you've ever felt nervous about starting a conversation because you're worried the other person will assume you're just trying to sell them something, you're not alone. But here's the good news: you can overcome this trust deficit by focusing on authenticity, sincerity and building genuine connections.

The Trust Deficit in MLM: How to Overcome It

Let's address the elephant in the room. MLM has, unfortunately, gained a reputation in some circles for being overly aggressive or transactional. Maybe you've encountered someone who sent a pitch within minutes of connecting on social media, or a friend who pushed a product on you at every opportunity. Experiences like these leave a bad taste and they can make people sceptical about anything related to MLM.

But here's the thing: *you are not those people*. And every interaction you have is an opportunity to rewrite the narrative, one conversation at a time.

Building trust starts with acknowledging this scepticism rather than ignoring it. For example, if someone says, "Oh, is this one of those MLM things?" instead of getting defensive, you could respond with honesty and a touch of humour: "Yes, it is, but I promise I'm not here to pressure you into anything! I genuinely think this might be helpful for you and I'd love to share more if you're open to it."

By being upfront and approachable, you immediately set yourself apart from the stereotypical MLM rep. You show that you respect the other person's boundaries and that your goal is to help, not to push.

Overcoming the trust deficit also means playing the long game. Trust isn't built overnight; it's the result of consistent actions over time. When you show up authentically, keep your promises and prioritise the relationship over the sale, you prove that you're someone worth trusting.

How to Convey Sincerity and Authenticity

Authenticity is one of those buzzwords that's easy to say but harder to practise, especially in MLM, where there's often pressure to "fake it till you make it." But the truth is, people can sense when you're being genuine—and when you're not. The key to conveying sincerity is to focus on connection rather than outcome.

Start by being yourself. If you're naturally bubbly and enthusiastic, let that shine through. If you're more reserved and thoughtful, embrace that too. There's no one-size-fits-all personality for success in MLM. The most important thing is that you're true to who you are.

For example, I once worked with a team member, Ben, who was soft-spoken and introverted. At first, he thought he needed to adopt a more outgoing persona to succeed, but it felt forced and awkward. When he started leaning into his natural strengths—listening carefully, asking thoughtful questions and building deeper connections—his business took off. People trusted Ben because he was authentic and that trust translated into sales and long-term relationships.

Another way to convey sincerity is to focus on the other person's needs rather than your own. Instead of thinking, *How can I sell to this person?* ask yourself, *How can I help them?* This mindset shift changes the tone of the conversation entirely.

For instance, if you're talking to someone who's mentioned they're struggling with low energy, don't immediately jump into a pitch about your product. Instead, ask questions like, "What's been working for you so far?" or "Have you tried anything else that's helped?" Listen to their responses and offer suggestions based on what you genuinely think will benefit them—even if it's not your product. When people feel heard and understood, they're more likely to trust you and your recommendations.

Real Stories of MLM Reps Who Built Trust the Right Way

To understand the power of trust in MLM, let's look at a couple of real-life examples of reps who got it right.

One of my favourite stories comes from Rachel, a mum of three who built her MLM business around skincare products. Rachel had a friend, Jess, who struggled with adult acne but was sceptical of MLMs due to a bad experience with a pushy rep in the past.

Instead of immediately trying to sell Jess something, Rachel took a different approach. She said, "I know you've had a bad experience before, so no pressure at all, but I've been using a product that's really helped me and I thought of you. Would you like to try a sample and see if it works for you?"

Jess appreciated Rachel's no-pressure approach and decided to give the sample a try. When it worked, she not only became a loyal customer but also started referring Rachel to her friends. Because Rachel prioritised trust over the immediate sale, she turned a sceptical friend into one of her biggest supporters.

Another inspiring story is about Tom, who was promoting health supplements. Tom's neighbour, Sam, had expressed interest but wasn't ready to commit. Instead of following up every week with, "Are you ready to buy yet?" Tom took a more thoughtful approach.

When he noticed Sam was training for a marathon, Tom sent him a message saying, "Hey Sam, I saw you're gearing up for the marathon—congrats! I've got a few tips on recovery that really helped me during my training. Let me know if you're interested."

Sam appreciated the gesture and the fact that Tom wasn't just trying to sell him something. Over time, they built a genuine friendship and when Sam finally decided to try the supplements, he was confident that Tom had his best interests at heart.

These stories highlight a simple truth: trust is built through small, consistent actions. It's about showing up, listening, and proving that you care more about the person than the sale.

Why Trust Matters in MLM

In MLM, trust isn't just about making a sale—it's about building relationships that last. When people trust you, they're more likely to listen to what you have to say, try your products and even recommend you to others.

But trust isn't something you can demand; it's something you earn. By acknowledging the trust deficit in MLM, approaching conversations with sincerity and authenticity, and focusing on connection over outcome, you can overcome scepticism and create meaningful relationships.

Building trust takes time, effort, and consistency, but it's worth it. Because when people trust you, they're not just buying a product—they're investing in you. And that's the foundation of a successful and sustainable MLM business.

Active Listening in Action

Have you ever been in a conversation where it felt like the other person wasn't really hearing you? Maybe they were nodding along but seemed distracted, or worse, they jumped in with a response before you'd even finished speaking. It's frustrating, isn't it? Now flip that around: how often do we, even with the best intentions, do the same thing?

In MLM, active listening is one of the most powerful tools you can use to build trust and rapport. It's about truly hearing what the other person is saying—not just their words, but the feelings and needs behind them. When done right, active listening doesn't just strengthen relationships; it also uncovers opportunities to help your prospects in meaningful ways.

The Three Levels of Listening

Listening isn't just about being quiet while the other person talks. There are different levels of listening and understanding these can help you become more intentional in how you engage with others.

1. **Surface Listening**
   At this level, you're hearing the words but not fully absorbing their meaning. You might nod and smile, but your mind is elsewhere—perhaps thinking about what you'll say next or even your to-do list.

For example, imagine someone tells you, "I've been so exhausted lately with work and the kids." If you're listening at the surface level, you might respond with something generic like, "Yeah, life can be so busy." While this isn't a bad response, it doesn't show that you've truly tuned in to their experience.

2. **Focused Listening**
   This is where you're giving your full attention to the person speaking. You're not just hearing their words; you're paying attention to their tone, body language, and emotions. At this level, you might respond to the same statement by saying, "That sounds exhausting. How are you managing to juggle everything?"

3. **Empathetic Listening**
Empathetic listening goes one step further. Here, you're putting yourself in the other person's shoes, imagining what it feels like to experience what they're describing. You're not just understanding their words; you're connecting with their emotions.

To the same comment, you might respond, "It must be really overwhelming trying to balance so much. I can only imagine how tired you must feel—how are you holding up?" This response not only shows understanding but also invites them to share more, deepening the connection.

In MLM, the goal is to operate at the focused or empathetic level as often as possible. When you listen deeply, people feel valued, heard and understood—key ingredients for building trust.

Practical Exercises to Improve Your Listening Skills

Listening is a skill and like any skill, it improves with practice. Here are a few exercises to help you sharpen your ability to listen actively:

1. **The 3-Second Rule**
Before responding in a conversation, pause for three seconds. This small delay helps ensure you're not just jumping in with a reflexive reply but actually processing what the other person has said.

For example, if someone shares that they've been struggling with their health, resist the urge to immediately suggest your product. Instead, take a moment to consider their words and ask a thoughtful follow-up question like, "What's been the hardest part for you?"

2. Mirror Their Words

After someone shares something, repeat or rephrase part of what they've said to show you've understood. For instance, if someone says, "I've been trying to eat healthier, but it's hard with my busy schedule," you could respond with, "It sounds like you're really committed to eating better, but time is a big challenge for you."

This technique not only confirms that you've heard them but also encourages them to elaborate further.

3. Tune Out Distractions

Active listening requires your full attention, which means minimising distractions. When you're having a conversation, put away your phone, make eye contact, and focus on the person in front of you. If you're on a call or a video chat, make sure you're in a quiet space where you can concentrate.

4. Practise Silence

One of the hardest parts of listening is resisting the urge to fill silences. But sometimes, a pause can encourage the other person to open up further. After asking a question, stay quiet and let them think. You might be surprised at how much they share when you give them the space to do so.

Real-Life Examples of Listening Uncovering a Key Need

Let's look at how active listening can uncover opportunities to help your prospects.

A team member of mine, Sarah, once had a conversation with a friend who was a new mum. During their chat, her friend mentioned feeling constantly tired and overwhelmed but didn't explicitly say she was looking for a solution. Instead of jumping in with a suggestion, Sarah asked, "What's been the hardest part of adjusting to life with a newborn?"

Her friend opened up about how she was struggling to find the energy to get through the day and felt like she wasn't taking care of herself. By listening empathetically and asking thoughtful questions, Sarah realised her friend wasn't just tired—she was craving something that would help her feel like herself again.

At that point, Sarah mentioned a supplement she'd been using that helped with energy and stress and because she'd taken the time to listen and understand, her friend didn't see it as a sales pitch—she saw it as a genuine suggestion from someone who cared.

Another example comes from Tom, who was promoting a fitness program. During a conversation with a work colleague, the colleague casually mentioned feeling frustrated about not being able to stick to a gym routine. Instead of immediately pitching the program, Tom said, "That sounds frustrating. What do you think makes it so hard to stick with it?"

His colleague shared that he hated how long gym sessions took and often felt out of place working out around younger, fitter people. This gave Tom the perfect opening to introduce his program, which focused on quick, at-home workouts. The colleague signed up, not because Tom pushed him into it, but because Tom listened and offered a solution tailored to his needs.

Why Listening Matters

Active listening isn't just a technique—it's a way of showing respect, empathy, and genuine care. When you listen deeply, you make the other person feel valued and understood, which is the foundation of trust.

In MLM, where trust is everything, listening can make or break a relationship. By practising the three levels of listening, honing your skills with simple exercises, and staying open to what your prospects are really saying, you'll not only strengthen your connections but also uncover opportunities to help in ways that truly resonate.

And here's the best part: when people feel heard, they're far more likely to listen to you in return. So, the next time you're in a conversation, take a deep breath, tune in, and let the other person's words guide the way. You might be surprised at what you discover.

Consistency and Follow-Through

If trust is the foundation of your MLM business, consistency and follow-through are the bricks that build it up. Trust isn't built in a single conversation or with a one-time gesture—it's established through small, meaningful actions repeated over time. In MLM, where relationships are everything, being reliable and consistent shows that you value the people you're connecting with and that they can count on you.

This section explores how simple, everyday actions can strengthen trust, how to avoid common follow-up mistakes and how thoughtful gestures—like remembering a birthday—can make all the difference in building lasting relationships.

Small Actions That Build Trust Over Time

Trust isn't about grand gestures or dramatic pitches; it's about showing up, day after day, in ways that demonstrate your sincerity and reliability. Often, it's the small actions—things that might seem insignificant—that have the biggest impact.

For example, if someone expresses interest in your product or business, a quick message a week later to check in shows that you're attentive and care about their experience. It doesn't have to be a formal follow-up; something as simple as, "Hi [Name], I was just thinking about you and wondered how you're going with [product/goal]. Let me know if there's anything I can help with!" can go a long way in showing you're not just in it for the sale.

Another small but powerful action is consistency in how you show up online. If you're using social media to connect with prospects, post regularly, engage with comments and respond to messages promptly. People notice when you're consistent, and it reinforces their confidence in you.

For instance, a friend of mine, Jess, built trust with her audience by sharing her journey with her MLM product in an authentic and consistent way. She didn't flood her feed with sales posts; instead, she sprinkled in updates about how the product was helping her, along with other content that showed her personality and values. Over time, her followers came to see her as genuine and relatable, which translated into increased engagement and sales.

Avoiding Common Follow-Up Mistakes

Follow-up is crucial in MLM, but it's also an area where many people trip up. One of the most common mistakes is following up too aggressively or too frequently. If someone isn't ready to make a decision, pushing them can feel invasive and might damage the relationship.

I learned this the hard way with a prospect named Megan. She'd expressed interest in joining my team but wanted time to think about it. I was so excited about the possibility that I messaged her every few days, asking if she'd made a decision. Eventually, Megan stopped responding altogether.

Looking back, I realised I'd been more focused on closing the deal than respecting her timeline.

Now, I follow a simple rule: if someone isn't ready, I give them space while still staying on their radar. For example, instead of asking, "Have you decided yet?" I might say, "Hi Megan, I just wanted to let you know we've got some great training resources available for new team members this month. Let me know if you'd like more info!" This approach keeps the door open without putting pressure on the prospect.

Another common mistake is failing to follow up at all. Life gets busy and it's easy to lose track of prospects, especially if you've got a long list. But if someone has expressed interest in your product or opportunity, a lack of follow-up can make them feel like you don't value their time or interest.

To avoid this, keep a simple system for tracking your follow-ups. Whether it's a spreadsheet, a CRM app, or even just a notebook, write down the date of your last interaction, what was discussed and when you plan to follow up next. This small habit ensures no one slips through the cracks.

How One Simple Act (Like Remembering Birthdays) Can Seal the Deal

Sometimes, it's the little, personal touches that leave the biggest impression. One of the easiest ways to show you care is by remembering special occasions, like birthdays.

I once had a prospect, David, who was interested in my MLM product but wasn't quite ready to commit. I knew his birthday was coming up because we were connected on Facebook, so I sent him a quick message: "Happy Birthday, David! I hope you have a fantastic day celebrating—you deserve it!"

It wasn't a sales message; it was just a genuine gesture to show I cared. David replied, thanking me and mentioning that he'd been thinking more about the product we'd discussed. That message opened the door to another conversation and within a week, he'd placed his first order.

Remembering birthdays, anniversaries, or even small details from past conversations—like their child's name or a recent holiday—can set you apart. It shows that you're paying attention and that your relationship with them is more than just transactional.

Another team member, Mia, takes this idea to the next level by sending handwritten thank-you notes to her customers after their first purchase. It's a simple gesture, but it leaves a lasting impression. One of her customers told her, "I've bought a lot of products online, but no one has ever taken the time to send a personal note before. It really means a lot." That customer not only became a repeat buyer but also referred Mia to several friends.

Small acts like these aren't difficult or time-consuming, but they have a way of turning prospects into loyal customers and even advocates for your business.

The Power of Follow-Through and Being Consistent

In MLM, building trust is a marathon, not a sprint. It's the result of small, consistent actions that show your prospects and customers you're reliable, attentive, and genuinely invested in their success.

By taking the time to follow up thoughtfully, avoiding common pitfalls and adding personal touches like remembering birthdays, you create a strong foundation of trust that can sustain your business for the long haul.

People don't just buy products or join teams—they buy into relationships. When you prioritise consistency and follow-through, you're not just building a business; you're building connections that last. And those connections are what truly make MLM a rewarding and fulfilling journey.

Chapter 4: Prospecting Online and Offline

Social Media Done Right

Social media has transformed the way we connect with people and for MLM, it's an incredibly powerful tool. But using social media effectively for prospecting isn't about spamming your followers with sales pitches or flooding your feed with product photos. It's about creating genuine connections, sharing value, and showing up as your authentic self.

When done right, social media allows you to reach your ideal audience, build trust and grow your business in ways that feel natural and engaging. Let's explore how to choose the right platforms for your niche, strike the perfect balance between personal and professional posts and implement strategies that actually work.

Choosing the Right Platforms for Your Niche

Not all social media platforms are created equal and the ones you focus on should depend on your niche and where your ideal customers spend their time.

For instance, if you're promoting health and wellness products, Instagram might be your best bet. It's a highly visual platform where people share their fitness journeys, recipes and lifestyle tips. By posting inspiring content and engaging with others in your niche, you can connect with an audience that values health and is open to trying new products.

On the other hand, if your business opportunity targets professionals looking for extra income or a side hustle, LinkedIn might be more effective. LinkedIn is a professional platform where people are already thinking about career growth and financial opportunities, making it a great place to start conversations about your business.

I remember working with Jacob, a team member who was struggling to gain traction on Facebook. He had a product that was tailored for young creatives and he felt like he wasn't reaching the right audience. After some brainstorming, we realised Instagram and TikTok were better fits for his him. Jacob started creating short, engaging videos showcasing his product in action and the response was incredible. By focusing on the platforms where his ideal customers were active, Jacob was able to grow his audience and make meaningful connections.

The key is to identify where your ideal customers are most active and invest your time and energy there. Trying to be everywhere at once can quickly become overwhelming and ineffective. It's better to focus on one or two platforms and do them well.

How to Balance Personal and Professional Posts

One of the most common mistakes people make when prospecting on social media is turning their profile into a billboard for their MLM business. While it's important to share your products and opportunities, it's equally important to let your personality shine through.

People connect with people, not brands. They want to see the real you—the mum juggling kids and a business, the fitness enthusiast passionate about health, or the coffee lover who can't function without a morning flat white. When you share a mix of personal and professional content, you create a well-rounded presence that feels relatable and authentic.

For example, if you're promoting skincare products, don't just post before-and-after photos or discount offers. Share your own skincare routine, talk about why you started using the products or post a funny video about the challenges of keeping up with self-care. Mix in personal content, like photos of your weekend adventures, a recipe you love, or a heartfelt post about a lesson you've learned in life or business.

A team member of mine, Claire, does this beautifully. She's a fitness coach who also promotes nutritional supplements. Her feed is a blend of workout tips, personal milestones and stories about her journey to better health. She regularly posts about her struggles and triumphs, which makes her audience feel like they know her—and more importantly, trust her. Because she balances personal and professional posts so well, her followers see her as a friend rather than someone constantly trying to sell something.

Examples of Successful Social Media Prospecting Strategies

So, how do you turn social media into a prospecting powerhouse? It starts with being intentional about how you engage with your audience. Here are some strategies that have worked for me and my team:

1. Start Conversations, Don't Sell
Instead of focusing on selling, focus on starting conversations. For example, if someone comments on your post about a healthy recipe, reply with a thoughtful message: "Thanks for your comment! Have you tried anything like this before? I'm always looking for new ideas." This approach keeps the conversation open and natural.

One of my team members, Tom, used this strategy to connect with a follower who commented on his post about energy-boosting tips. They chatted about shared struggles with fatigue, which eventually led to a discussion about

Tom's product. The follower became a loyal customer, not because Tom pushed the product but because he listened and offered a solution.

2. Use Stories to Build Connections
Instagram and Facebook Stories are perfect for sharing behind-the-scenes glimpses of your life and business. Use them to show your day-to-day activities, highlight your product in action, or share tips related to your niche.

For example, if you're promoting eco-friendly cleaning products, you could post a Story showing how quick and easy it is to clean your kitchen with your favourite product. Add a poll sticker asking, "Do you love eco-friendly products?" to spark engagement.

I've personally found Stories to be a great way to connect with people. One day, I shared a Story about my morning routine, including the health drink I use. A friend replied, asking what it was, which led to a conversation and eventually a sale. Stories feel less formal than posts, making them a great space for organic interactions.

3. Leverage Groups and Communities
Joining groups or communities related to your niche can help you connect with like-minded people. For example, if you're promoting weight loss products, join a Facebook group for people on fitness journeys. But remember, the goal is to contribute value, not to spam the group with ads.

A team member of mine, Rachel, joined a local mums' group on Facebook. She regularly shared tips about meal prepping and managing busy schedules, which aligned perfectly with her health-focused MLM products. Over time, group members started reaching out to her for advice and many became customers. Rachel's success came from genuinely engaging with the group and building relationships before mentioning her products.

4. Follow Up with Intentionality
Social media prospecting doesn't end with a comment or a like—it's about following up in meaningful ways. For instance, if someone watches your Stories consistently or engages with your posts, send them a friendly message: "Hi [Name], I noticed you've been following my health tips. Thanks so much for your support—it really means a lot. Is there anything you'd like to know more about?"

One of the best follow-ups I've seen came from a team member, Liam, who reached out to a follower who had commented on his post about meal replacement shakes. Instead of jumping into a sales pitch, Liam asked, "I saw your comment—are you looking for new ideas for quick meals? I've been experimenting with some recipes lately and would love to share!" This approach led to a conversation, trust, and eventually a sale.

The Power of Social Media Done Right
Social media isn't about chasing likes or followers—it's about creating connections and building relationships. By choosing the right platforms, balancing personal and

professional content and using intentional strategies, you can turn your social media presence into a powerful tool for prospecting.

The most important thing is to be yourself. Show up authentically, share your story and engage with your audience in meaningful ways. When you do, social media stops feeling like a chore and starts becoming a space where your business—and your relationships—can thrive.

Offline Opportunities

While social media has transformed the way we connect, offline prospecting remains just as powerful—and sometimes even more so. There's something irreplaceable about face-to-face interactions. The warmth of a smile, the energy of a shared laugh and the personal connection that comes from looking someone in the eye can set the foundation for meaningful relationships.

The beauty of offline opportunities is that they're everywhere. Whether you're at a networking event, chatting with someone in a coffee shop or bumping into an old friend at the park, there are countless chances to start conversations that could lead to new relationships—and new business opportunities.

Networking Events: How to Work the Room with Ease

Networking events can be intimidating, especially if you're not naturally outgoing. The thought of walking into a room full of strangers and striking up conversations might make your palms sweat. But with a little preparation and the right mindset, networking events can become one of your most effective tools for prospecting.

The key to working the room is to focus on connection rather than self-promotion. Instead of worrying about pitching your product or business, approach each interaction with curiosity. Your goal isn't to "sell" but to meet people, learn about them and plant the seeds for future conversations.

I remember my first big networking event vividly. I was nervous and unsure how to start conversations, so I hung back near the coffee table for far too long. But then I decided to focus on listening rather than talking. I walked up to someone standing alone and simply said, "Hi, I'm [Your Name]. What brought you here today?" That one question opened the door to an engaging conversation and by the end of the night, I'd made several meaningful connections.

Here are a few tips that have worked well for me:

- **Arrive early.** It's easier to strike up conversations when the room isn't packed.
- **Have an icebreaker ready.** A simple question like, "What do you do?" or "How did you hear about this event?" can start a conversation naturally.

- **Listen more than you speak.** People love talking about themselves, so ask questions and let them share their story.
- **Don't rush to pitch.** If the opportunity arises, great, but don't force it. Focus on building rapport first.

By the end of a networking event, your goal should be to leave with a few meaningful connections rather than trying to talk to everyone. Follow up with those you've connected with—whether it's a quick email, a LinkedIn message, or a coffee invite—and nurture those relationships over time.

Everyday Moments: Turning Casual Chats into Opportunities

Prospecting doesn't have to be confined to formal events or scheduled meetings. Some of the best opportunities happen in the most unexpected places: at the gym, waiting in line at the supermarket or even chatting with another parent at school pickup.

The trick to turning everyday moments into opportunities is to be genuinely curious about the people around you. Instead of seeing each interaction as a potential sale, view it as a chance to connect and learn about someone's story.

One of my favourite examples comes from a team member, Lisa, who met a new customer while waiting for her coffee at a local café. She noticed the woman in front of her was juggling a pram and several bags, so she offered to help. They struck up a conversation, and Lisa asked, "How's your day going?" The woman shared that she was exhausted and struggling to keep up with her busy schedule. Lisa empathised and mentioned a product she'd been using that had helped her feel more energised. They exchanged numbers and that casual chat turned into a lasting customer relationship.

Another example is my own experience at the gym. I'd been attending a yoga class regularly and over time, I got to know one of the other participants, Sarah. One day, she mentioned feeling stuck in her fitness journey and I shared how a product I used had helped me. As we'd already built rapport through our shared yoga practice, the conversation felt natural and unforced—and Sarah ended up becoming one of my most loyal customers.

The key to turning casual chats into opportunities is to listen for cues. When someone mentions a challenge or need that aligns with what you offer, it's an opening to share your story or product in a way that feels helpful rather than pushy.

A Checklist for Being Prepared to Prospect Anytime, Anywhere

Opportunities to prospect can arise when you least expect them, so it's important to be prepared. Here's a simple checklist to ensure you're always ready:

1. **Know Your Elevator Pitch**
   Have a concise, natural way to describe what you do

or the product you offer. For example: "I help people find simple, sustainable ways to boost their energy and feel their best." Keep it conversational and avoid jargon.

2. **Carry Business Cards or Samples**
You never know when someone will express interest, so having something to give them—a business card, a sample, or even just your contact details—can make a big difference.

3. **Be Ready with Stories**
Stories are powerful tools for connection. Think about a few personal or customer success stories that illustrate the value of your product or opportunity.

4. **Stay Positive and Approachable**
People are drawn to positivity, so smile, make eye contact and show genuine interest in others.

5. **Have Follow-Up Tools Handy**
Whether it's a notebook, your phone, or a contact app, have a way to jot down details about new connections so you can follow up later.

6. **Practice Active Listening**
Pay attention to what people are saying, ask thoughtful questions, and look for opportunities to offer value.

Being prepared doesn't mean you need to be "on" all the time. It's about having the tools and mindset to recognise and seize opportunities when they naturally arise.

The Power of Offline Opportunities

While online prospecting has its place, there's something uniquely powerful about face-to-face connections. Whether you're working the room at a networking event, striking up a conversation in your everyday life or simply staying open to the people around you, offline opportunities can help you build trust and rapport in ways that are hard to replicate online.

The key is to approach each interaction with curiosity, authenticity, and a genuine desire to connect. When you focus on building relationships rather than chasing sales, you'll find that offline prospecting becomes less about "selling" and more about creating meaningful connections that grow your business naturally.

So, take a deep breath, smile and start a conversation—you never know where it might lead.

Blending Online and Offline

In the world of MLM, the most successful prospecting strategies often blend the best of both worlds: online and offline. While social media allows you to reach people quickly and efficiently, offline interactions bring the personal touch that builds trust and rapport. When these approaches work together, they create a seamless process for building relationships, nurturing leads and growing your business.

This section explores how online tools can enhance your offline interactions, shares a real-life example of combining both strategies effectively and highlights how tools like CRM software can help you track and manage your efforts.

Using Online Tools to Enhance Offline Interactions

Online tools are incredibly useful for staying connected and organised, but they're even more powerful when used to complement your offline efforts. Think of online tools as bridges that extend the reach of your face-to-face connections, allowing you to maintain and deepen relationships long after the initial interaction.

For example, let's say you meet someone at a networking event. You have a great conversation and they express interest in your product. Instead of relying solely on a business card exchange, connect with them on LinkedIn, Facebook, or Instagram. By following up with a thoughtful message—like "It was great meeting you at [event]! I really enjoyed our chat about [topic]. Let's stay in touch"—you keep the relationship warm and give them a way to learn more about you.

Social media is also an excellent way to share value with your offline connections. If you've met someone who's interested in health and fitness, you can send them a link to a recent post or video you've shared about tips or success stories in that space. This not only provides value but also positions you as someone knowledgeable and helpful in your niche.

Another example is using email to follow up after an offline meeting. A simple, personalised email thanking someone for their time and sharing additional resources—like a blog post, a product brochure or even a personal testimonial—can keep the conversation going.

Real-Life Example of Combining Both Approaches Effectively

A friend of mine, Sarah, runs a successful MLM business promoting natural skincare products. One day, she met a woman named Emma at a yoga class. They struck up a conversation about their favourite self-care routines and Emma mentioned she was looking for more natural alternatives for her skincare.

Sarah didn't launch into a sales pitch right then and there. Instead, she asked Emma if she'd like to connect on Instagram, where Sarah often shared tips and ideas about skincare. Emma agreed, and over the next few weeks, Sarah noticed Emma engaging with her posts—liking photos, commenting on stories and asking questions about the products Sarah used.

When Sarah followed up with Emma offline during another yoga class, the conversation felt natural and unforced. Sarah offered Emma a sample of her favourite moisturiser and because Emma already trusted her and had seen how passionate Sarah was about the products online, she decided to make a purchase.

This combination of an offline introduction and online nurturing turned a casual conversation into a loyal customer relationship.

What made Sarah's approach work was her focus on connection. By combining offline warmth with online engagement, she created a consistent and trustworthy presence that made Emma feel comfortable taking the next step.

Leveraging Tools Like CRM Software for Better Tracking

One of the challenges of blending online and offline prospecting is keeping track of your interactions. With so many conversations happening in different places—social media, email, phone calls, in-person events—it's easy for details to slip through the cracks.

This is where CRM (Customer Relationship Management) tools can be a game-changer. CRM software helps you organise and track your leads, so you always know where you are in the prospecting process. It allows you to store contact details, notes from conversations and follow-up reminders all in one place, making it easier to manage your growing network.

For example, let's say you meet someone at a coffee shop who's interested in your product. Using a CRM tool, you can log their name, the date you met, and any details they shared about their needs or interests. You can also set a reminder to follow up with them in a week, ensuring you don't forget about the opportunity.

I use a simple CRM tool for my own MLM business and it's made a huge difference in how I stay organised. One time, I met a woman named Jackie at a local community event. She mentioned she was looking for ways to boost her energy levels but wasn't ready to buy anything right away. I added her details to my CRM and set a follow-up reminder for two weeks later.

When I reached out, I was able to reference our previous conversation, saying, "Hi Jackie, I hope you're doing well! Last time we spoke, you mentioned you were looking for ways to feel more energised. I just came across a new article about energy-boosting tips and thought of you—would you like me to send it your way?"

Jackie appreciated the follow-up and eventually became a customer—not because I pushed her but because I showed I cared and stayed consistent.

Bringing It All Together

Blending online and offline prospecting isn't about choosing one approach over the other—it's about integrating them to create a seamless experience for your prospects. Use online tools to stay connected and share value, and let offline interactions bring the personal touch that builds trust.

By following up thoughtfully, using social media strategically and leveraging tools like CRM software, you can keep your network warm, organised, and engaged.

Remember, every interaction—whether it's online or offline—is an opportunity to show up authentically, listen to your prospects' needs and offer value. When you combine the strengths of both approaches, you create a prospecting process that's not only effective but also enjoyable—for you and the people you connect with.

Chapter 5: Handling Objections Like a Pro

Understanding Objections

When you're prospecting in MLM, objections are part of the game. They're not just inevitable—they're a sign you're actively putting yourself out there and having real conversations. Yet, hearing someone say "no" or "I'm not interested" can still sting, especially if you've poured your heart into building trust and sharing what you genuinely believe can help them.

But here's the truth: objections aren't personal. They're simply a natural part of decision-making. In fact, they often mean the other person is considering what you're offering—they just need more clarity, confidence, or time to take the next step.

By understanding the psychology behind objections, learning to differentiate between genuine concerns and smoke screens and reframing how you respond, you'll find that objections can actually be opportunities to connect deeper and help your prospects move closer to a "yes."

The Psychology Behind Common Objections

When someone raises an objection, it's easy to assume they're shutting you down. But more often than not, objections are rooted in deeper feelings like uncertainty, fear or a desire for control. Understanding what's really driving these responses can help you approach them with empathy and confidence.

For instance, when a prospect says, "I don't have the money," what they might really mean is, "I'm not sure this is worth the investment." Similarly, "I don't have the time" often translates to, "I'm not sure this fits into my priorities right now."

These objections are less about the specific product or opportunity and more about how it aligns with their current circumstances and values. When you recognise this, you can shift your focus from convincing them to understanding their perspective and addressing their underlying concerns.

I remember speaking with a friend, Jake, about joining my MLM business. When he said, "I don't think I have the time for this," my initial reaction was to feel a bit deflated. But instead of ending the conversation, I asked, "What does your schedule look like at the moment?" Jake opened up about juggling work, family and a side hustle. By listening, I learned that his concern wasn't about time itself—it was about feeling overwhelmed and unsure how he could take on something new.

By reframing objections as opportunities to learn more about your prospects, you create space for deeper, more productive conversations.

Differentiating Between Genuine Concerns and Smoke Screens

Not all objections are created equal. Some are genuine concerns that need addressing, while others are smoke screens—a polite way of saying, "I'm not ready" or "I'm not interested." The challenge is figuring out which is which so you can respond appropriately.

Genuine concerns often come with a specific reason or question. For example, "I don't know if I can afford this" might be followed by questions about pricing or payment options. These are invitations to provide more information and help your prospect make an informed decision.

On the other hand, smoke screens tend to be vague or surface-level. If someone says, "I'll think about it" but doesn't engage further, they might be trying to end the conversation without hurting your feelings.

One way to differentiate between the two is to ask clarifying questions. For example, if a prospect says, "I'm not sure this is for me," you might respond with, "That's completely fine—can I ask what's holding you back?" If they share a specific concern, it's likely genuine. If they brush it off or avoid getting into details, it might be a smoke screen.

I once had a prospect, Claire, who said, "I need to think about it." Instead of pushing for a commitment, I replied, "Of course. Is there anything you'd like to know more about while you're deciding?" Claire admitted she wasn't clear on how much time the business would require. By addressing that concern, I was able to help her see how she could fit it into her life—and she eventually joined my team.

Remember, your role isn't to force anyone into a decision but to guide them with clarity and empathy. By being patient and asking thoughtful questions, you'll build trust and uncover the real barriers to their "yes."

How Not to Take Objections Personally

Rejection can feel personal, especially in MLM, where you're not just promoting a product—you're sharing something you're passionate about. But here's the truth: when someone says "no" or raises an objection, it's not about you. It's about their circumstances, priorities, or preferences at that moment.

Understanding this can take the sting out of objections and help you approach them with a clearer mindset. It's not always easy, but reframing how you view rejection can make all the difference.

I'll never forget a conversation I had early in my MLM journey. I was talking to a long-time friend, Terry, about a product I thought he'd love. When he said, "I'm not interested," I felt crushed. I started doubting myself, thinking, *Did I come on too strong? Does he not trust me?*

But later, I learned that Terry had just gone through a tough financial patch and wasn't in a position to spend money on anything non-essential. His "no" wasn't about me or the product—it was about his situation. Realising this helped me let go of the idea that every objection was a reflection of my abilities.

One way to handle objections without taking them personally is to focus on the bigger picture. For every "no," there's a "yes" waiting around the corner. Objections are part of the process, not the end of it.

Another tip is to view each objection as a learning opportunity. Ask yourself, *What can I take away from this interaction?* Maybe you'll learn how to communicate more effectively, address concerns more proactively, or refine your approach for next time.

For example, a team member of mine, Rachel, shared how she used to feel devastated whenever someone rejected her product. But instead of giving up, she started keeping a journal of her conversations. After each interaction, she'd jot down what went well, what didn't, and what she could improve. Over time, Rachel noticed patterns—like the importance of building rapport before diving into a pitch—and her confidence grew.

Turning Objections into Opportunities

Objections might feel like roadblocks, but they're often stepping stones. When you approach them with empathy, curiosity and resilience, they become opportunities to build trust, understand your prospects better and refine your approach.

Remember, objections aren't personal—they're part of the journey. By understanding the psychology behind them, recognising the difference between genuine concerns and smoke screens and reframing your response, you'll not only handle objections more effectively but also strengthen your relationships and grow your business with confidence.

So, the next time you hear a "no," take a deep breath, smile, and remember: it's not about rejection—it's about redirection.

Reframing Objections

Objections can feel like the end of the road in a conversation, but they're often just detours. Many people say "no" as an initial reaction—not because they're completely uninterested, but because they need more information, reassurance, or time. The key is learning how to reframe objections in a way that keeps the conversation open and productive.

Reframing doesn't mean arguing or pressuring someone into changing their mind. It's about showing empathy, addressing their concerns and guiding them toward a new perspective. In this section, we'll explore the "Feel-Felt-Found" approach, how to turn a "no" into "not now," and the importance of asking clarifying questions.

The "Feel-Felt-Found" Approach in Action

The "Feel-Felt-Found" approach is a classic but powerful way to reframe objections because it validates the other person's concerns while gently offering a new perspective. It works by acknowledging their feelings, sharing a similar experience and presenting a solution that worked for you or others.

Here's how it looks in practice: Imagine someone says, "I'm not sure I can afford this right now."

Using the "Feel-Felt-Found" method, you might respond: "I completely understand how you feel. When I first heard about this, I felt the same way—I was worried about spending money on something new when I wasn't sure it would work. But what I found was that after trying it, it saved me money in other areas because it replaced a few products I was already using. If it makes sense for you, I'd love to help you figure out if this could work in your budget too."

This response shows empathy (you understand their hesitation), relates to their experience (you felt the same way), and offers a solution (what you found after giving it a chance). It doesn't dismiss their concern; it respects it while opening the door for further discussion.

A friend of mine, Claire, used this approach when a prospect was hesitant about joining her team, saying, "I'm not sure I'm confident enough to do this." Claire replied, "I know how you feel. I felt the same way when I started—I wasn't sure if I had the confidence or the skills. But what I found was that the training and support from the team made a huge difference, and I learned as I went. I'd love to support you the same way if you decide to give it a try."

The prospect appreciated Claire's honesty and ended up joining the team because she felt reassured and understood.

Examples of Turning "No" into "Not Now"

Not every "no" is permanent. Sometimes, people just need more time, information, or the right circumstances before they're ready to say "yes." Reframing "no" as "not now" helps you keep the relationship warm and the door open for future opportunities.

Take Sarah, for instance. She approached a colleague, James, about trying her wellness product. James said, "Thanks, but I don't think it's for me." Instead of seeing this as a dead end, Sarah replied, "That's totally fine, James. If you ever change your mind or want to learn more, just let me know—I'd be happy to help."

Two months later, James reached out to Sarah after hearing a coworker talk about the same product. He said, "I've been feeling really low on energy lately and I remembered our chat. Can we revisit it?"

By keeping the conversation open and respectful, Sarah turned what initially seemed like a firm "no" into a future "yes."

Another example comes from my own experience. I had a prospect, who was interested in joining my team but said, "I just don't think I have the time right now." Instead of trying to convince them otherwise, I said, "I completely understand, life gets so busy! If it's okay with you, I'll check in a few months down the track to see if things have changed for you."

They really appreciated the no-pressure approach. When I followed up three months later, their schedule had eased, and they were ready to join.

Reframing "no" as "not now" requires patience and a long-term perspective. It's about respecting the other person's timeline while staying consistent and available.

The Power of Asking Clarifying Questions

One of the best ways to reframe objections is by asking clarifying questions. When someone raises a concern, it's tempting to jump in with a solution—but taking a moment to dig deeper can uncover the real issue and help you respond more effectively.

For example, if someone says, "I don't think this is for me," you might ask, "What makes you feel that way?" This simple question invites them to share their thoughts and gives you valuable insight into their concerns.

I once had a prospect, David, who said, "I don't think I'd be any good at this." Instead of trying to convince him otherwise, I asked, "What do you think would be the biggest challenge for you?" David admitted he was worried about not knowing how to talk to people or make sales. This gave me the opportunity to share how our team provides training and support and he ended up feeling confident enough to give it a try.

Another time, a customer told me, "I'm not sure this product will work for me." Instead of defending the product, I asked, "What makes you unsure?" The customer explained that they'd tried similar products before without success. This allowed me to share a specific story about how the product had helped someone in a similar situation, which eased their doubts and led to a sale.

Clarifying questions not only help you understand the objection better—they also show the other person that you're genuinely interested in their concerns and not just focused on making a sale.

Reframing Objections: A Skill Worth Mastering

Reframing objections is one of the most valuable skills you can develop in MLM. By using the "Feel-Felt-Found" approach, recognising that "no" often means "not now" and asking thoughtful clarifying questions, you can transform objections from roadblocks into opportunities for deeper connection and trust.

Remember, objections aren't the end of the conversation—they're an invitation to keep exploring. When you approach them with empathy, curiosity, and a willingness to listen, you'll find that many "no's" eventually turn into "yeses."

Most importantly, reframing objections shows your prospects that you're there to help, not to pressure. And when people feel respected and supported, they're far more likely to engage with you—not just as a businessperson but as someone they trust and value.

Closing Without Pressure

Closing a prospecting conversation is often the most nerve-wracking part of the process. After all, you've put in the effort to build trust, address objections and show how your product or opportunity can help. The last thing you want is to come across as pushy or ruin the connection you've worked so hard to create.

The good news is that closing doesn't have to feel like a high-pressure sales tactic. In fact, the most effective closings are often subtle and collaborative, allowing the prospect to feel in control of their decision. By letting them set the pace, using gentle guidance, and staying true to your integrity, you can close conversations with confidence and grace.

How to Let the Prospect Lead the Pace

One of the biggest mistakes in closing is rushing the process. If someone feels pushed into making a decision before they're ready, it can create resistance or even end the relationship entirely. Instead, let the prospect set the pace and focus on meeting them where they are.

For example, if a prospect says, "I need a bit more time to think about it," respect their timeline. Instead of pressing them for an immediate answer, respond with something like, "Of course—take all the time you need. Is there any additional information I can share to help you decide?" This approach shows that you value their decision-making process and aren't just chasing a sale.

I remember working with a prospect, Kate, who was interested in joining my team but wasn't sure if the timing was right. Rather than trying to convince her to join immediately, I said, "Kate, this opportunity will always be here, so don't feel pressured to rush. I'd love to stay in touch and answer any questions as they come up." A month later, Kate reached out to say she was ready to join because she felt supported rather than pressured.

Letting the prospect lead the pace requires patience, but it also builds trust and ensures that their decision is genuinely theirs—a key ingredient for long-term success.

Subtle Techniques for Guiding the Conversation Toward a Yes

While it's important to let the prospect lead, you can still gently guide the conversation toward a positive outcome. The key is to be subtle and supportive, helping them see how your product or opportunity aligns with their needs and goals.

One effective technique is to ask open-ended questions that encourage the prospect to imagine the benefits of saying yes. For example, if someone is hesitant about trying your product, you might ask, "How would it feel to have more energy during the day?" or "What would it mean for you to finally find a solution that works?" These questions shift the focus from hesitation to possibility, making the decision feel more empowering.

Another subtle technique is to use assumptive language. This doesn't mean assuming the sale but rather framing your statements in a way that reinforces the value of moving forward. For instance, instead of saying, "Do you want to try this?" you might say, "When you're ready to get started, I'll make sure you have all the support you need." This creates a sense of partnership and confidence without being pushy.

A friend of mine, Liam, used this approach beautifully when working with a prospect who was interested in his fitness program but hesitant to commit. Liam said, "I think you'd love this program—it's perfect for someone with your goals. If you decide to give it a go, I'd be happy to help you customise it to fit your routine." By focusing on collaboration and support, Liam made the prospect feel confident and valued, which led to a successful close.

Success Stories of Closing with Confidence and Integrity

Some of the best closing stories come from moments when reps focused on helping rather than selling, allowing the prospect to make the decision on their own terms.

One of my team members, Rachel, had a prospect, Sophie, who was interested in her skincare line but hesitant about the price. Instead of pushing Sophie to buy, Rachel said, "I completely understand—it's an investment, and I want you to feel confident about it. Would it help if I shared a bit more about how to get the most value out of the product?" Sophie appreciated Rachel's patience and decided to purchase, knowing she had Rachel's guidance to make the most of her investment.

Another example comes from Tom, who was promoting his MLM business opportunity. He was speaking with a prospect, David, who loved the idea of earning extra income but was nervous about his lack of experience. Instead of trying to "sell" the opportunity, Tom said, "David, I see so much potential in you, but this has to feel right for you. If you decide to join, I'm here to support you every step of the way—but if now isn't the time, that's okay too."

David later told Tom that this no-pressure approach was what made him feel comfortable joining. He knew Tom genuinely cared about his success, not just signing him up.

These stories highlight an important truth: closing isn't about "sealing the deal" at all costs—it's about creating a positive experience that leaves the prospect feeling confident, respected and excited about their decision.

The Power of Closing Without Pressure

When you approach closing with patience, empathy and a genuine desire to help, it becomes less about convincing and more about collaborating. By letting the prospect set the pace, using subtle techniques to guide the conversation and focusing on integrity, you can create closing experiences that feel natural and rewarding for both you and the prospect.

Remember, the goal isn't to force a "yes"—it's to build relationships and trust that lead to mutual success. When you close without pressure, you're not just gaining a customer or team member—you're creating a partnership that's built to last.

Chapter 6: Maintaining Momentum and Growing Your Network

The Power of Follow-Up

Follow-up is where the magic happens in MLM. It's the bridge between an initial conversation and a meaningful connection, whether that connection turns into a sale, a new team member or a loyal advocate for your business. Yet, follow-up is often overlooked or avoided, largely because it can feel awkward or intrusive.

The truth is, most people won't say "yes" the first time you introduce them to your product or opportunity. That doesn't mean they're not interested—it just means they need more time, information or encouragement to make a decision. Consistent, thoughtful follow-up is what turns those "maybes" into "yeses," but only if it's done the right way.

In this section, we'll explore how to follow up effectively without coming off as a nuisance, and I'll share some real-life success stories to show how powerful follow-up can be.

Turning "Maybe" Into "Yes" Through Consistent Touchpoints

Imagine planting a seed in your garden. You don't just plant it and walk away, expecting it to grow on its own. You water it, make sure it gets enough sunlight, and tend to it over time. Follow-up works the same way. That initial conversation is the seed and your consistent touchpoints are the care it needs to grow into something meaningful.

I remember one of my first experiences with follow-up. I'd spoken to a friend, Jess, about a skincare product I was promoting. She seemed interested but said, "Let me think about it." In the past, I might have taken that as a polite way of saying no and moved on. But instead, I decided to follow up.

A week later, I sent Jess a message: "Hi Jess, I was just thinking about you and wondering if you had any questions about the skincare product we talked about. No rush—just wanted to make sure you had all the info you needed."

Jess replied, thanking me for checking in and mentioned she'd been meaning to ask about the ingredients. That follow-up led to another conversation and eventually, Jess decided to try the product.

The key to effective follow-up is to stay on their radar without being pushy. It's about showing that you care and are genuinely interested in helping them, rather than just making a sale.

Consistent touchpoints can take many forms:

- A quick message to check in.
- Sharing an article or resource that's relevant to their interests.
- Letting them know about a special offer or promotion.

Each touchpoint is a gentle reminder that you're there to support them whenever they're ready.

How to Avoid Coming Off as a Nuisance

One of the biggest fears people have about follow-up is being perceived as a nuisance. No one wants to be that person who constantly pesters others or makes them feel pressured. The good news is, with the right approach, follow-up can feel helpful and respectful rather than intrusive.

The first rule of thumb is to always leave the ball in their court. For example, instead of saying, "Are you ready to buy yet?" you might say, "I just wanted to check in and see if there's anything else you'd like to know about [product]. Let me know if or when you're ready to chat more!"

This approach gives the prospect the space to make their own decision while keeping the lines of communication open.

Timing also matters. If someone says they need a week to think it over, respect that timeline and don't follow up before it's over. After that, a simple, friendly message like, "Hi [Name], I hope you're doing well! I just wanted to follow up and see if you've had a chance to think more about [product/opportunity]" can go a long way.

Another way to avoid coming off as a nuisance is to add value with each touchpoint. Instead of just checking in, share something useful or relevant to their interests. For example, if you're promoting health supplements and know the prospect is interested in fitness, you might send them a link to an article about workout nutrition. This shows that you're thinking about their needs, not just your business.

I once had a prospect, Emma, who was hesitant about joining my MLM team. During our conversations, she mentioned feeling overwhelmed by the idea of learning sales skills. When I followed up, instead of asking if she'd made a decision, I sent her a free resource about effective communication techniques, saying, "Hi Emma, I came across this and thought it might be helpful based on our chat. Let me know what you think!" Emma appreciated the gesture, and it helped build her confidence enough to eventually join the team.

Examples of Follow-Up Success Stories

One of the best things about follow-up is that it can lead to incredible success stories—sometimes in the most unexpected ways.

A friend of mine, Tom, shared a great example. He'd spoken to a colleague, Ben, about a product that helped with stress and focus. Ben was curious but non-committal, saying, "I'll think about it." Instead of letting the conversation end there, Tom made a note to follow up two weeks later.

When he did, he kept it casual: "Hi Ben, I hope things are going well! I just wanted to check in and see if you had any questions about [product]. No pressure—just thought I'd touch base."

It turned out that Ben had forgotten about the product in the midst of a busy work schedule but was still interested. The follow-up reminded him and he decided to give it a try. Not only did Ben become a loyal customer, but he also referred Tom to a few friends who were experiencing similar stress challenges.

Another success story comes from Rachel, who was promoting a fitness program. She'd met a potential customer, Sarah, at a local event and followed up with a quick message: "Hi Sarah, it was great chatting with you at [event]! I remember you mentioned wanting to find something that fits into your busy schedule—would you like me to share more about how [program] works?"

Sarah appreciated the follow-up but wasn't ready to commit at the time. Over the next few months, Rachel stayed in touch by sending occasional tips about quick workouts and healthy recipes. Eventually, Sarah decided to sign up, saying, "You've been so helpful and I feel like I can trust you to guide me through this."

These stories highlight the power of persistence, patience and thoughtful follow-up. By staying connected and adding value, you can turn initial interest into lasting relationships.

The Power of Follow-Up

Follow-up isn't just a task on your to-do list—it's a vital part of building trust, nurturing relationships and growing your business. When done with care and intention, it shows your prospects that you value them as individuals, not just potential sales.

By turning "maybe" into "yes" through consistent touchpoints, respecting their timeline, and adding value with each interaction, you can create follow-up experiences that feel genuine and productive. And as the success stories show, a simple follow-up can sometimes lead to incredible outcomes.

So don't shy away from follow-up. Embrace it as an opportunity to deepen your connections, provide support, and show that you're in it for the long haul. After all, the best relationships—and the best businesses—are built one conversation at a time.

Building Referrals

Referrals are the hidden gems of MLM. A single referral can open the door to a whole new network of potential customers or team members, often with much less effort than cold prospecting. Why? Because people trust recommendations from friends, family and colleagues more than a stranger's pitch.

But referrals don't just happen—they need to be nurtured. The good news is, when you make it easy for others to refer you, recognise their efforts, and show gratitude, you'll create a ripple effect that can grow your business exponentially.

How to Make It Easy for Others to Refer You

The first step to building referrals is to ensure the process is simple and stress-free. If people feel like referring you will be a hassle or that they need to do all the work, they're unlikely to follow through.

Start by being clear about what you're looking for. Let your customers and team members know exactly who you help and how they can make an introduction. For example, if you're promoting health supplements, you might say, "If you know anyone who's been looking for a natural way to boost their energy, I'd love to chat with them." This gives them a specific idea of who might benefit from your product or opportunity.

I once had a loyal customer, Emma, who loved the wellness products I was promoting but hadn't thought about referring anyone. When I mentioned, "Emma, you've been such a fan of these products—if you know anyone who might enjoy them too, feel free to send them my way," she immediately thought of her sister, who ended up becoming a customer.

Another way to make referrals easy is to provide tools and resources. For instance, you can give your customers a short message they can send to their friends or a link to your website. This removes any guesswork and makes the process seamless.

One team member of mine, Rachel, created a referral card with her contact details and a brief description of her product. She gave these cards to her customers and encouraged them to pass them along to anyone who might be interested. The result? Several new customers reached out to Rachel, saying they'd heard about her through a friend.

Rewarding and Recognising Referrals

People are more likely to refer you if they feel appreciated for their efforts. Rewarding and recognising referrals not only encourages more referrals but also strengthens your relationships with your customers and team members.

Rewards don't have to be extravagant—a small token of appreciation can go a long way. For example, you might offer a discount, a free sample or a personalised thank-you note for every successful referral. The key is to show genuine gratitude and make the referrer feel valued.

I once ran a referral program where customers who referred a friend received a small gift—a sample of a new product or a discount on their next purchase. One customer, Lisa, referred three friends in one month because she loved the idea of trying new products for free.

Recognition is just as important as rewards. Publicly acknowledging someone's referral efforts can make them feel proud and appreciated. For example, if you have a private customer group on social media, you could post a shout-out: "A huge thank-you to Sarah for introducing her friend to [product]! Your support means the world to me."

Real-Life Examples of Referrals Growing an MLM Business Exponentially

Referrals have the potential to transform your MLM business in ways that can feel almost magical. A single referral can lead to a chain reaction, connecting you to new networks and opening doors you never even knew existed.

Take the story of Claire, one of my most successful team members. Claire had a customer, Emily, who loved her skincare products. When Emily's friend complimented her glowing skin, she immediately referred her to Claire. That friend became a customer and later referred two more people, both of whom joined Claire's team. Over the course of a year, that one initial referral snowballed into a network of 15 new customers and three team members.

Another inspiring example comes from my own experience. I once worked with a customer, David, who was passionate about health and fitness. I asked him, "David, you know so many people in the fitness community—if anyone mentions they're looking for ways to boost their performance, would you mind sending them my way?" David agreed and introduced me to his trainer, who loved the product and started recommending it to his clients. That single introduction led to a surge in sales and a new partnership that boosted my business for months.

These stories highlight the exponential power of referrals. When someone refers you, they're not just connecting you to a single person—they're opening up their entire network, giving you access to opportunities you might never have found on your own.

The Power of Building Referrals

Building a strong referral network is one of the most effective ways to grow your MLM business. By making it easy for others to refer you, showing genuine appreciation for their efforts and celebrating their contributions, you create a cycle of trust and goodwill that benefits everyone involved.

Referrals aren't just about growing your customer base—they're about building relationships and creating a community of people who believe in what you do. And when you approach referrals with authenticity and gratitude, you'll find that your network grows not just in size, but in depth and loyalty as well.

So, don't be afraid to ask for referrals. Make it easy, rewarding, and meaningful, and watch as your business thrives from the power of genuine connections.

Keeping the Spark Alive

Building an MLM business is an exciting journey, but it's not without its challenges. The early days are often filled with enthusiasm as you connect with new prospects, celebrate your first wins and start to see the potential of what you're building. But as time goes on, it's normal to experience dips in motivation, moments of doubt or even burnout.

Keeping the spark alive in your MLM journey is crucial—not just for your business but for your overall wellbeing. By preventing burnout, celebrating small wins and staying consistent, you can maintain momentum and continue to thrive, even when the going gets tough.

Preventing Burnout in Prospecting

Burnout can creep in when you're constantly pushing yourself without taking time to rest, recharge or reflect. In MLM, where success often depends on consistent effort, it's easy to feel like you have to be "on" all the time. But trying to do everything at once can leave you feeling drained and disconnected from the passion that brought you into this business in the first place.

One of the best ways to prevent burnout is to set realistic goals and boundaries. Instead of aiming to connect with 50 new prospects in a week, focus on quality over quantity. Set a goal to have meaningful conversations with five people instead. This allows you to give each interaction your full attention without overwhelming yourself.

I remember a time when I was pushing myself too hard, spending hours every day messaging people and attending back-to-back meetings. I started to dread prospecting and felt like I was losing the joy I'd once had for the business. A mentor of mine gave me some simple but powerful advice: "You can't pour from an empty cup. Take care of yourself first."

I started scheduling breaks, setting specific work hours and giving myself permission to step away from the business when I needed to recharge. The result? I felt more energised and my conversations became more genuine and effective.

Another key to preventing burnout is finding ways to make prospecting enjoyable. If you love coffee, set up meetings at your favourite café. If you're active on social media, incorporate prospecting into your daily scrolling by engaging with people who genuinely interest you. When you align your prospecting activities with what you enjoy, it feels less like work and more like an extension of your lifestyle.

Celebrating Small Wins to Stay Motivated

In MLM, it's easy to focus on the big goals—hitting a sales milestone, earning a promotion or growing your team. While these achievements are worth striving for, it's just as important to celebrate the small wins along the way.

Every time you connect with a new prospect, follow up with a lead, or receive positive feedback from a customer, you're making progress. These small wins might seem insignificant in the moment, but they're the building blocks of long-term success.

I remember one of my team members, Rachel, who was feeling discouraged because she hadn't signed up a new customer in weeks. We sat down to look at what she had accomplished and it turned out she'd started five meaningful conversations, followed up with three prospects and received glowing feedback from a long-time customer. None of these were big, headline-grabbing wins, but they were proof that she was moving in the right direction.

To help Rachel stay motivated, we created a simple habit: every Friday, she'd write down three wins from the week, no matter how small. Over time, this practice helped her stay positive and focused and it wasn't long before those small wins led to bigger successes.

Celebrating small wins can be as simple as treating yourself to a coffee after a productive day, sharing your progress with a supportive friend or mentor, or keeping a journal of your achievements. The more you recognise and appreciate your efforts, the more motivated you'll feel to keep going.

Stories of MLM Reps Who Thrived by Staying Consistent

Consistency is the secret sauce in MLM. It's not about doing everything perfectly but about showing up day after day, even when it feels challenging. The reps who thrive are the ones who keep going, even when progress feels slow or setbacks arise.

One of my favourite examples is Tom, a team member who started his MLM journey with no prior experience in sales. In his first few months, Tom faced rejection after rejection. He often joked, "I've probably heard 'no' more times in the past three months than in my entire life." But instead of giving up, Tom committed to staying consistent.

He made it a habit to reach out to five new prospects every week, no matter what. Some weeks were better than others, but Tom focused on the process rather than the results. Slowly but surely, his efforts started to pay off. After six months, Tom had built a loyal customer base and recruited his first team member. By the end of his first year, he'd earned a promotion and was mentoring others on the importance of consistency.

Another inspiring story comes from Claire, who built her MLM business while working full-time and raising two young children. Claire didn't have hours to dedicate to prospecting, but she made the most of the time she had. Every day during her lunch break, she spent 30 minutes connecting with prospects online or following up with leads.

Claire's progress was steady but slow at first, and there were times when she doubted whether her efforts would pay off. But she stuck with it, celebrating each small win along the way. After a year of consistent effort, Claire had built a thriving business that allowed her to reduce her hours at work and spend more time with her family.

These stories show that consistency isn't about doing everything all at once—it's about doing something, every day, that moves you closer to your goals.

The Power of Keeping the Spark Alive

Building an MLM business is a marathon, not a sprint. There will be highs and lows, moments of doubt and periods where progress feels slow. But by preventing burnout, celebrating small wins, and staying consistent, you can maintain your momentum and keep the spark alive.

Remember, the journey is just as important as the destination. Every conversation, follow-up, and connection is a step toward building something meaningful—not just a business, but a network of relationships and a life you're proud of.

So, take a deep breath, smile, and keep going. The spark that inspired you to start this journey is still there, and with care and consistency, it will continue to light the way.

Conclusion: Prospecting with Purpose

Building a successful MLM business is more than just selling products or recruiting team members—it's about creating genuine connections, adding value to people's lives and staying true to your purpose. Prospecting isn't simply a task to check off your to-do list; it's the heart of your business and a powerful opportunity to make a positive impact on others.

Throughout this book, we've explored practical strategies, relatable stories, and actionable techniques to help you approach prospecting with confidence and integrity. Let's take a moment to reflect on the key lessons we've covered, the importance of authenticity, and how you can start putting everything into practice right away.

Key Lessons from the Journey

From understanding your ideal customer to mastering the art of follow-up, each chapter has provided tools and insights to support your prospecting journey.

We began by focusing on the foundation of all successful prospecting: knowing your ideal customer. By defining who they are, researching their needs and building a vivid customer avatar, you've learned how to approach the right people with the right message.

Next, we explored how to start conversations with confidence—whether online, offline or a blend of both. You've discovered the power of active listening, the importance of small talk, and the value of consistent follow-through to build trust and rapport.

In the chapters on handling objections, we shifted perspectives, recognising that objections are not roadblocks but opportunities to understand your prospects better and guide them toward a decision that feels right for them.

Finally, we focused on momentum and growth, exploring how to maintain motivation, build referrals and keep the spark alive in your business.

These lessons aren't just strategies—they're the building blocks of a sustainable and fulfilling MLM journey.

The Importance of Authenticity and Relationship-Building

If there's one overarching theme throughout this book, it's the power of authenticity. People don't join businesses or buy products—they connect with people. They're drawn to your story, your energy and your genuine desire to help.

Authenticity means showing up as your true self, whether you're sharing your story online, chatting with someone at a café or following up with a prospect. It means being honest about your intentions, listening more than you speak and prioritising relationships over transactions.

Building strong, lasting relationships is the key to success in MLM. When people trust you and feel valued, they're more likely to become loyal customers, refer others to you and even join your team. And as your network grows, so does the ripple effect of your impact.

A great example of this is a team member of mine, Lisa, who built her business around her passion for wellness. Lisa never approached conversations with a sales pitch; instead, she focused on sharing her story and listening to others. Over time, her authenticity attracted a community of like-minded people who trusted her and were eager to support her business.

This is what it means to prospect with purpose: connecting with others in a way that feels meaningful, genuine and aligned with your values.

Your Action Plan: Putting It into Practice

Now that you've learned the principles and strategies of effective prospecting, it's time to take action. Here's a simple plan to help you start implementing these techniques immediately:

1. **Define Your Ideal Customer**
   Take a few minutes to review the customer avatar you created earlier in this book. Are there any details you can refine? Use this profile as your guide to focus your prospecting efforts on the people most likely to benefit from what you offer.

2. **Start Conversations Today**
   Challenge yourself to have at least three meaningful conversations this week. Whether online or offline, focus on connecting authentically and learning about the other person's needs. Remember, it's not about making a sale—it's about starting a relationship.

3. **Follow Up with Purpose**
   Identify three people you've already spoken to but haven't followed up with yet. Send them a thoughtful message to check in, share value, or answer any questions they might have.

4. **Ask for Referrals**
   Reach out to your existing customers or contacts and let them know how much you appreciate their support. Ask if they know anyone who might benefit from what you offer and make the referral process as easy as possible for them.

5. **Celebrate Your Wins**
   At the end of each week, take a moment to reflect on your progress. Write down your wins—no matter how

small—and celebrate the effort you're putting into building your business.

By taking these simple steps, you'll start to see the principles of this book come to life in your daily prospecting efforts.

Prospecting with Purpose: A Final Thought

Your MLM journey is uniquely yours, shaped by your passion, goals and the connections you make along the way. Prospecting isn't just about growing your business—it's about growing yourself, building relationships and creating a ripple effect of positive impact.

As you move forward, remember that every conversation is an opportunity. Whether it leads to a sale, a new team member, or simply a meaningful connection, each interaction brings value. And with every step you take, you're not just building a business—you're building a community.

So go out there and prospect with purpose. Be authentic, stay consistent and focus on making a difference. The results will come, but more importantly, you'll create a business—and a life—you're truly proud of.

Resource Section: Practical Tools for Your MLM Journey

This section is packed with tools to make your MLM prospecting easier and more personal. These templates and scripts are designed to help you build genuine connections, follow up with confidence and grow your business without feeling pushy. Adapt them to suit your style and use them as a guide to get started.

1. Social Media Post Templates

A. Sharing Your Journey

Purpose: Share your personal story to inspire others.

Example:
"When I first started using [product name], I wasn't sure what to expect. But over time, it's completely changed my life. Whether it's [benefit one] or [benefit two], I've noticed such a difference. I know it might not be for everyone, but if you're curious about how it works, let's have a chat. I'd love to share my experience."

B. Highlighting a Product

Purpose: Gently showcase a product you love.

Example:
"Who else feels like they're always running on empty? For me, [product name] has been a game-changer. Whether I'm [specific activity] or just trying to get through the day, it's made such a difference. If you're curious about [key benefit], I'm happy to answer any questions or share more info."

C. Asking an Engaging Question

Purpose: Start a conversation with your audience.

Example:
"If you could fix one thing in your daily routine—whether it's feeling more energised, having better focus or getting a bit of 'me time'—what would it be? I've been working on some small changes myself and would love to hear what you're trying."

D. Keeping It Real

Purpose: Share a slice of your life while mentioning your business.

Example:
"Life's a bit of a juggle at the moment—between work, the kids' sport and keeping up with [activity], it can feel like there's no time for myself. I'm so glad I've got [product name]

in my corner. It's the little things that make a big difference. What's helping you get through the chaos?"

2. Follow-Up Message Templates

A. Reaching Out After Your First Chat

Purpose: Reconnect and show you care.

Example:
"Hi [Name], I hope you're doing well! I just wanted to follow up about [product/opportunity] and see if you had any questions. No rush—just wanted to check in and let you know I'm here if you need anything."

B. Checking In After Sharing Information

Purpose: Keep the conversation going naturally.

Example:
"Hi [Name], I wanted to see if you had a chance to look over the [sample/brochure/info] I sent. Let me know if there's anything I can help with or clarify!"

C. Friendly Reminder

Purpose: Stay top of mind without being overbearing.

Example:
"Hi [Name], I know life gets busy, so I thought I'd quickly

check in about [product/opportunity]. No pressure at all—just wanted to see if you're still interested or if you have any questions."

D. After a "No" or "Not Now"

Purpose: Leave the door open for future opportunities.

Example:
"Hi [Name], thanks for letting me know where you're at. If things change or you ever want to revisit [product/opportunity], just give me a shout. No pressure at all—I'm always here to help."

3. Scripts for Conversations

A. Starting a Conversation

Purpose: Break the ice without sounding rehearsed.

Example:
"Hi [Name], it's been a while—how have you been? I saw your post about [topic] and thought of you. How's everything going with [related detail]?"

B. Introducing a Product

Purpose: Share your product naturally during a chat.

Example:

"You mentioned [challenge/goal] earlier and I couldn't help but think of [product name]. It's been such a help for me with [specific result] and I thought it might be worth a chat to see if it's something you'd find useful."

C. Talking About the Business Opportunity

Purpose: Introduce the opportunity without sounding pushy.

Example:

"Hi [Name], I was thinking about our chat the other day. You mentioned [specific goal] and I thought what I'm working on could be a great fit for you. Would you like me to tell you more? No pressure at all—I just thought it might be worth a look."

D. Handling Objections

Purpose: Address concerns with empathy and honesty.

Example:

"I totally get where you're coming from—I felt the same way at first. But what I found was that [specific reassurance]. If you're interested, I'd be happy to share more or help you figure out if it's the right fit."

4. Tools to Stay Organised

A. Follow-Up Tracker

Use a simple table or notebook to keep track of your conversations. Here's an example layout:

Name	Date of Contact	Notes from Chat	Next Follow-Up	Status
Jane Doe	5 Feb 2024	Interested in skincare	12 Feb 2024	Sent info, follow-up scheduled

B. Digital Tools

If you prefer digital tools, try:

- **Google Sheets**: Perfect for a simple, customisable tracker.
- **Trello**: Great for visualising where prospects are in your pipeline.
- **HubSpot CRM**: A free option for more advanced tracking.

5. Referral Scripts

A. Casual Referral Request

Purpose: Encourage happy customers to refer others.

Example:
"Hi [Name], I'm so glad you're enjoying [product]! If you know anyone who might love it too, feel free to send them my way. I'd really appreciate it and would be happy to help them out."

B. Referral Program Invitation

Purpose: Offer an incentive for referrals.

Example:
"Hi [Name], I'm starting a little thank-you program for referrals! If you refer a friend who tries [product], you'll receive [reward, e.g., a discount, free sample]. Let me know if there's anyone you'd like me to chat with!"

6. Celebrate Wins and Stay Motivated

Weekly Wins Journal

At the end of each week, jot down:

1. One meaningful conversation you had.
2. One follow-up you completed.
3. One new connection you made.

Example Entry:

- Connected with Sarah about [product].

- Followed up with Dave about joining the team.

- Chatted with Claire at the gym—she's curious about [product].

These tools and templates are here to help you take action. Adjust them to sound like you, keep the focus on building relationships and remember to enjoy the journey. With every conversation, follow-up and referral, you're building something meaningful. Go for it—you've got this!

www.ingramcontent.com/pod-product-compliance
Lightning Source LLC
Chambersburg PA
CBHW071034240526
45469CB00006BD/2209